# British and Irish Silver Assay Office Marks

## 1544 - 1963

with notes on Gold Markings, and
Marks on Foreign Imported Silver
and Gold Plate.

## Old Sheffield Plate Makers' Marks

### 1743-1860

Compiled by

FREDERICK BRADBURY, F.S.A
SHEFFIELD, England

Author of
*History of Old Sheffield Plate*
*Antique Silver, &c.*

Eleventh Edition, 1964
(Copyright)

J. W. Northend Ltd.
*Printers and Publishers*
West Street, Sheffield 1
England

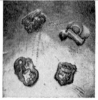

SILVER-GILT CUP AND COVER
by Paul Lamerie

bearing London Assay Mark
date 1739

*In the collection of the*
*Worshipful Company of Goldsmiths*
*by whose kind permission it is here printed*

# CONTENTS

## MINOR GUILDS

# PREFACE

The Assay Marks depicted in this small work of reference have been collected for a period of over 60 years, assembled and noted at various times by the Author and others who have collaborated with him. They have been submitted for investigation to various well known collectors, also the Masters who have held office at the various Assay Offices in England, Scotland, and Ireland.

Other sources have been searched for knowledge in connection with articles bearing provincial Assay Marks met with from time to time and of which very little definite information has been recorded.

As this work is published in the form of a handy reference book only, should the reader require more definite particulars concerning the origin, styles and workmanship of the craftsmen associated with the production of Antique Silver, he will find the following published works of great assistance to him: *English Goldsmiths and their Marks*, by the late Sir Charles J. Jackson, F.S.A., and *The Illustrated History of English Plate*, by the same author. *The Gold and Silver of Windsor Castle: Old Plate of the Cambridge Colleges: Old Silver, European & American, etc.*, by E. Alfred Jones, M.A., F.S.A., F.R.Hist.S., many volumes by the Rev. J. T. Evans, M.A., F.S.A., on *Church Plate*, and *English & Scottish Silver Spoons* by Com. G. E. P. How, R.N., also *English Church Plate* and *English Domestic Silver* by Charles Oman, *Silver* by Gerald Taylor (Pelican) and the V. and A. Museum Handbooks on Silver. Other authors who have written notable works dealing with the subject of Antique Silver are:— Wilfred J. Cripps, C.B., F.S.A., W. W. Watts, F.S.A., Octavius Morgan and W. Chaffers.

*For assistance accorded in
the tabulation of the marks produced in
this small work, the
Author desires to thank the following
gentlemen for the services they have rendered*

Mr. A. Westwood - - - Birmingham
Mr. Hamil Westwood (Assay Master)
Birmingham
Mr. Llewellyn Davies - - - Cardiff
Mr. Fred Lowe - - - - Chester
Mr. G. W. Thornley (Pres., Assay Office) Dublin
Mr. Ronald le Bas (Assay Master) Dublin
Mr. G. W. M. Crichton (Assay Master)
Edinburgh
Mr. C. Biggs - - - - - Exeter
Mr. E. Walker (Assay Master) - Glasgow
Messrs. Christie, Manson & Woods - London
Mr. L. Crichton - - - - London
Mr. J. J. Hodges - - - - London
Com. G. E. P. How, R.N. - - - London
Mr. E. Alfred Jones - - - London
Mr. A. J. Koop (V. & A. Museum) - London
Mr. G. R. Hughes - - - - London
Mr. W. A. Prideaux, *Clerk*, Mr. J. S. Forbes, *Dep. Warden, Wor. Company of Goldsmiths* London
Mr. C. W. Oakford - - Philadelphia, U.S.A.
Mr. E. Senior Atkin - - - Sheffield
Mr W. P. Belk - - - - Sheffield
Mr. W. F. Northend, F.S.A. - Sheffield
Mr. W. Sissons - - - - Sheffield
Mr. W. T. Cocks (Assay Master) Sheffield
Revd. J. T. Evans - Stow-on-The-Wold
Mr. H. G. Baker - - - Swinton, Yorks.
Mr. Arthur J. Hawkes, F.S.A. - Wigan
Major H. N. Robertson - Wrotham, Kent

# INTRODUCTION

*An explanation of the Assay Offices devices
used in Great Britain and Ireland*

Those who have formed a comprehensive collection of Old English Silver Plate have an advantage in that their acquisitions can be accurately dated and the source of origin located by the series of Hall Marks shown on each article in their possession.

From the end of the 12th century the craft of the silversmith has been regulated in conformity with Royal Ordinances and Acts of Parliament, consequently, most articles of silver plate bear marks which enable the year, the place of assay and also the maker's name to be definitely traced. Names registered before the end of the 17th century, however, cannot be identified from marks owing to the plates having been destroyed at the London Goldsmiths' Hall in the Great Fire of 1666. In England, the craft was regulated by the Guild of Goldsmiths at London; in Scotland, by the Guild at Edinburgh, and in Ireland, by the Guild at Dublin.

The experience gained by centuries of investigation has resulted in the evolution of a complete system of Hall Marking. The same purpose was served at each office by striking a mark, similar in character though different in detail. These marks constitute

## MAKER'S MARK

The maker's mark. Until early in the 17th century a symbol. From 1696-1720, the first two letters of surname were frequently used with symbol, and occasionally, in the late 17th

6

century, makers used a rebus of their names as a mark. After 1720, usually letters only to identify the maker.

John Buck                                    T. Dove

The makers' marks struck on antique silver of all periods are far too numerous to be dealt with in a small work of this description, but it is notable that there are records of Goldsmiths' names to be found dating back to the early years of the Norman Conquest, whilst in the latter part of the 12th century, a "Guild" or association of Goldsmiths and Silversmiths was existing in London.

## MARK OF ORIGIN

The mark of origin, differing at each assay office, was first introduced in London towards the end of the 14th century; this enables the location of the office of assay to be traced.

Edinburgh          London          Dublin

## DATE LETTER

A letter of the alphabet enables the year of assay to be assigned. This letter was changed each year and varied in form or the outline of its shield at the beginning of each cycle of letters.

## ASSAY MARK

The Lion Passant was first used in the year 1544 as a device, when silver was assayed, to indicate that the metal was of sterling quality.

7

Earlier than this, specimens of the craftsmen's work are extremely scarce, but in the publications referred to specimens are dealt with which have a traceable history in connection with the oldest British Assay Offices dating back to the 14th century.

On examining these early specimens it will be observed that owing to the efflux of time the marks to be seen thereon are usually somewhat worn and indistinct, nevertheless, initials and devices of that period, which are decipherable, can be relied on as an elucidation of the origin of silver articles produced in the Middle Ages.

The Lion Passant was not adopted by the English Provincial Assay Offices as a device until 1719. In that year, by Act of Parliament, the 92.5 per cent sterling standard for wrought silver plate was restored after a lapse of 22 years, during which period the standard had been raised to 95.8 per cent fine, commonly described as the Britannia Standard.

## DUTY MARK

The Sovereign's Head shows that duty has been paid on the piece bearing it. It appears on all articles made between December 1st 1784 and April 30th 1890, except on those articles not liable to compulsory hallmarking and on watchcases after 1798. During that period a tax, varying from time to time, was levied on all silver assayed in Great Britain. At the Dublin Assay Office the Sovereign's head as Duty Mark was not introduced until 1807, and at Glasgow until 1819.

## BRITANNIA DEVICE

In 1696, the conversion of Silver Coin into Plate so interfered with the trade of the Country that an Act was passed raising the standard of Wrought Plate from 925 parts of pure silver to 958 per thousand. The marks of the Leopard's Head and Lion Passant were withdrawn and the Lion's Head erased and Figure of Britannia substituted. The Lion's Head erased

shows that the article was assayed in London. The Figure of Britannia that it was of the "new" or higher standard. The use of this standard was compulsory until 1720, after which date it became optional and is still used occasionally today, being distinguished by the Britannia mark together with the Assay Office mark of one or other of the existing assay offices.

## JUBILEE MARK

A mark bearing the heads of King George V and Queen Mary was used to commemorate the 25th Anniversary of their Accession and may be found on silver plate for the years 1933-4-5.

## CORONATION MARK

Bearing the head of Queen Elizabeth II. Used on silver plate assayed in 1953 to commemorate the Accession of Her Majesty. As most of the Assay Offices do not change the date letter until about the middle of the year plate bearing the letter for 1952 will be found with the Coronation Mark as well as 1953.

 LONDON

THIS small book begins with the London Assay Office marks, whilst those used by other offices follow alphabetically. Examples of every known type of silver plate, both decorative and useful, are to be found assayed in London. The Guild mark depicts the Leopard's Head, which varies in aspect from time to time, and is surmounted with a Crown between the years 1478 and 1821 since which date the crown has been deleted.

The London Silversmiths have maintained a very high standard of design and workmanship throughout the centuries of the establishment of their Guild, whilst the more notable craftsmen have shown individuality in the conception and execution of their designs to an extent which has won the world's admiration.

## BIRMINGHAM

THIS Office, established by Act of Parliament in 1772, was opened in 1773. Its distinguishing mark is an Anchor which is accompanied by a Lion Passant, a date letter, duty mark (Sovereign's Head) and maker's initials. Antique Silver of Birmingham origin is confined chiefly to the smaller class of goods, viz: vinaigrettes, snuff boxes, buckles, gun furniture and other small wares, with only a limited quantity of domestic plate.

## CHESTER

A GUILD of Goldsmiths supervised the manufacture, assay and sale of plate in this city as early as the beginning of the 15th century, but the marking was not regulated until towards the close of the 17th century. The marks then used were similar to those found on London

Hall marked silver of the same period, and the sequence of date letters followed in alphabetical order. The distinguishing mark is a shield bearing the Arms of the city. Antique Silver Plate with the Chester mark thereon is more or less confined to smaller articles in the form of Tankards, Beakers, Tumbler Cups, Pipkins and Cream Jugs. It does not embrace the whole range of the silversmith's craft. The Chester office was closed down 24th August, 1962.

# DUBLIN

THE Hall Marking of Irish Silver began towards the middle of the 17th century. The mark of origin is the Harp Crowned and it appears with a date letter and maker's mark. In 1731, the figure of Hibernia was added. The whole range of the silversmith's craft is to be found bearing the Dublin assay marks: the workmanship was excellent, but the designs were usually of a decorative nature. Dublin absorbed many emigrant goldsmiths after the revocation of the Edict of Nantes in 1685 and their influence can be distinctly traced in the production of Irish Silver of the 18th century

# EDINBURGH

ANTIQUE Silver bearing Scottish Hall Marks has been found as early as the middle 16th century. The oldest specimens portray, as a mark of origin, "The Castle" of Edinburgh City which is accompanied by the Deacon's (or Assay Master's) mark and also the maker's initials. The first sequence of date letters begins with the year 1681 and is arranged alphabetically. The device of a Thistle was introduced in 1759 to replace the Deacon's Mark, and is still to be found on all Silver Plate bearing the Edinburgh Hall Marks. The whole range of domestic and ecclesiastical plate was manufactured in the capital city from the earliest times, and shows great individuality in its conception, For much information in connection with Scottish Hall Marks, thanks are due to Commander G. E. P. How, R.N.

# EXETER

SILVER Plate was made in this ancient city from the very earliest times, and the assay marks date from the middle of the 16th century. The mark of origin was in the form of a letter X usually in a round shield surmounted by a Crown. In 1701 this was replaced by a three-towered Castle. Assay marking was conducted somewhat irregularly until the beginning of the 18th century. From 1701-1720, in addition to the town and makers' marks, the Britannia mark and Lion's Head erased in vogue at other assay offices were used, and these, after 1721, gave place to the Leopard's Head and Lion Passant in square shields.

Much fine plate was made in Exeter, notably, Ecclesiastical Vessels, Tankards, Loving Cups,

Caudle Cups and Covers, Coffee Pots and Tea Pots, but very few of the small articles are to be found bearing the Exeter assay marks. There is documentary evidence that late in the 17th century a large number of craftsmen dwelt in the city, but at the end of the 18th century the assaying of silver in Exeter was of a very perfunctory nature, though the right of Hall marking was exercised intermittently until the year 1882 after which date it ceased entirely.

# GLASGOW

SILVER appears to have been first assayed in this city during the last quarter of the 17th century. The mark of origin is a Tree with a Bird in its upper branches, a Bell suspended from a lower branch, and a Fish laid at the base. This device was accompanied by a sequence of date letters. In 1819, the Lion Rampant of Scotland and the Sovereign's Head were added.

Silver plate bearing the early Glasgow Hall Marks is very scarce. The Glasgow Assay Office was closed down on 31st March, 1964.

# NEWCASTLE-ON-TYNE

SILVER was assayed here from the middle of the 17th century. The town mark was three separate Castles in a shield but the marking was erratic until 1702, when the figure of Britannia and Lion's Head erased, denoting the new Standard, were first introduced. In 1720, on the restoration of old standard, the Leopard's Head and Lion Passant were substituted for these two marks and were used with town mark and date letter. The Lion Passant faces to the right from 1721 to 1727.

Much silver was assayed in Newcastle during the early part of the 18th century, chiefly of a domestic kind, such as Coffee Pots and Tea Pots, a particular feature being the large quantity of Tankards and Two-handled Cups produced in this town

# NORWICH

SILVER was made in the city from very early times, and assay marks can be traced to the middle of the 16th century, when the mark of origin was a Castle surmounting a Lion Passant used with a date letter and maker's mark.

In the first quarter of the 17th century a further town mark was added, viz: a Seeded Rose Crowned. During the last half of the century this was altered to a Rose with a stem. Silver marking was very erratic at this office, and little, if any, silver was assayed after 1701. Some fine examples, made in Norwich, are to be found in the Eastern Counties confined chiefly to church and corporation plate

# SHEFFIELD

THIS Office, established by Act of Parliament in 1772, was opened in 1773. The mark of origin is the Crown accompanied by the usual sequence of marks in use at other assay offices. A peculiarity of the office was an association in one punch of a date letter and crown between the years 1780 and 1853. The date letters began in 1773 with the letter E, and were varied irregularly each year until 1824, after which date they were arranged in alphabetical order. All forms of decorative and domestic plate in use during the 18th and 19th centuries are to be found bearing Sheffield Hall Marks. An important feature of the production of Sheffield silversmiths was the making of Candlesticks. Numbers of these were purchased by the London and Edinburgh Silversmiths who, even subsequent to the establishment of Sheffield Assay, continued to imprint their marks and caused those of their respective offices to be superimposed thereon.

1775
Sheffield Hall Marks.

1775
Sheffield marks overstruck at Goldsmiths' Hall, London.

1790
Sheffield marks overstruck at Edinburgh Assay Office.

# YORK

SILVER was assayed in this old Yorkshire capital from the middle of the 16th century. The mark of origin was a halved Leopard's Head with a Fleur-de-lis similarly treated conjoined in one shield. This was used with a sequence of date letters and maker's marks. Towards the end of the 17th century the half Leopard's Head was replaced by a half Seeded Rose. In 1701 the town mark was altered to Five Lions Passant on a Cross. Early pieces of plate made in the city were of fine design and workmanship, closely resembling those of Scandinavian origin, and consist largely of ecclesiastical and domestic plate, notably Caudle Cups and Tankards, both with and without covers. Only a very small number of silver articles were assayed in York between 1700 and 1780, and from 1780 till the close of the office in 1856, those produced were of a very ordinary description and more for domestic use.

# MINOR GUILDS

Taunton          Cork          Greenock

ONLY the more important Guilds of Minor Goldsmiths who assayed their silver locally are tabulated in this book. Their productions were chiefly confined to the making of spoons, which bore a device or initials in repetition more frequently than marks of origin.

16

*Dates of Accession of Sovereigns of England, showing
the main changes in Assay Marks of
the London Office from 1509 and when introduced.*

Principal Changes

| Henry VIII | . | . 1509 |
| Edward VI | . | 1547 |
| Mary I . | . | . . 1553 |
| Elizabeth I | . | 1558 |
| James I | . | . . 1603 |
| Charles I | . | . . 1625 |
| Commonwealth | | 1649 |
| Charles II | . | . 1660 |
| James II | . | . . 1685 |
| William III and Mary II . | | . 1689 |
| William III . | | . 1695 |

1697 Britannia Standard

| Anne . | . | . . 1702 |
| George I | . | . . 1714 |

1720 Old Standard Restored

| George II | . | . 1727 |
| George III | . | . 1760 |

1784 Duty Mark (Sovereign's
head) incuse

1786 Duty Mark in cameo

| George IV | . | . 1820 |

17

1821 Leopard's Head
uncrowned

William IV . . 1830

Victoria . . . 1837

1890 Duty Mark ceased

Edward VII . . 1901
George V . . 1910

1933-4-5 Jubilee Mark

Edward VIII . 1936
George VI . . 1936

1953 Coronation Mark

Elizabeth II . . 1952

1954

FOR assistance accorded in compilation of this work, the author was indebted to Captain S. W. Turner, M.C., F.R.S.A., Freeman of the Goldsmiths' Company of London and the Cutlers' Company of Sheffield, also to Mr. G. H. Eno of Sheffield and Mr. Dudley Westropp of Dublin

| | | | |
|---|---|---|---|
| Henry VIII 1544 | | G | |
| 1545 | | H | |
| 1546 | ,, | I | ,, |
| Edw VI 1547 | ,, | K | ,, |
| 1548 | ,, | L | |
| 1549 | ,, | M | ,, |
| 1550 | ,, | N | |
| 1551 | | O | |
| 1552 | ,, | P | |
| Mary 1553 | ,, | Q | ,, |
| 1554 | ,, | R | ,, |
| 1555 | ,, | S | ,, |
| 1556 | ,, | T | ,, |
| 1557 | ,, | V | |

# LONDON

| | | | | | |
|---|---|---|---|---|---|
| **Elizabeth** 1558 | a | 1578 | A | 1598 | A |
| 1559 | b | 1579 | B | 1599 | B |
| 1560 | C | 1580 | C | 1600 | C |
| 1561 | d | 1581 | D | 1601 | D |
| 1562 | e | 1582 | E | 1602 *Jas 1* 1603 | E F |
| 1563 | f | 1583 | F | 1604 | G |
| 1564 | g | 1584 | G | 1605 | h |
| 1565 | h | 1585 | H | 1606 | I |
| 1566 | i | 1586 | I | 1607 | K |
| 1567 | k | 1587 | K | 1608 | L |
| 1568 | l | 1588 | L | 1609 | M |
| 1569 | m | 1589 | M | 1610 | N |
| 1570 | n | 1590 | N | 1611 | O |
| 1571 | o | 1591 | O | 1612 | P |
| 1572 | p | 1592 | P | 1613 | Q |
| 1573 | q | 1593 | Q | 1614 | R |
| 1574 | r | 1594 | R | 1615 | S |
| 1575 | s | 1595 | S | 1616 | T |
| 1576 | t | 1596 | T | 1617 | V |
| 1577 | u | 1597 | V | | |

| | | | | | |
|---|---|---|---|---|---|
| 1618 | ⓐ | 1638 | ⓐ | 1658 | ⓐ |
| 1619 | ⓑ | 1639 | ⓑ | 1659 Chas. II. | ⓑ |
| 1620 | ⓒ | 1640 | ⓒ | 1660 | ⓒ |
| 1621 | ⓓ | 1641 | ⓓ | 1661 | ⓓ |
| 1622 | ⓔ | 1642 | ⓔ | 1662 | ⓔ |
| 1623 | ⓕ | 1643 | ff | 1663 | ⓕ |
| 1624 Chas. I. | ⓖ | 1644 | ⓖ | 1664 | ⓖ |
| 1625 | ⓗ | 1645 | ⓗ | 1665 | ⓗ |
| 1626 | ⓘ | 1646 | ⓘ | 1666 | ⓘ |
| 1627 | ⓚ | | | 1667 | ⓚ |
| 1628 | ⓛ | 1647 | ⓑ | | |
| 1629 | ⓜ | 1648 Comwth. | ⓔ | 1668 | ⓛ |
| 1630 | ⓝ | 1649 | ⓨ | 1669 | ⓜ |
| 1631 | ⓞ | 1650 | ⓝ | 1670 | ⓝ |
| 1632 | ⓟ | 1651 | ⓧ | 1671 | ⓞ |
| 1633 | ⓠ | 1652 | ⓟ | 1672 | ⓟ ⓟ |
| 1634 | ⓡ | 1653 | ⓠ | 1673 | ⓠ |
| 1635 | ⓢ | 1654 | ⓡ | 1674 | ⓡ |
| 1636 | ⓣ | 1655 | ⓢ | 1675 | ⓢ |
| 1637 | ⓥ | 1656 | ⓣ | 1676 | ⓣ |
| | | 1657 | ⓤ | 1677 | ⓤ |

21

# LONDON

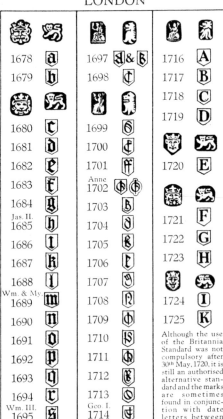

| Year | Mark | Year | Mark | Year | Mark |
|------|------|------|------|------|------|
| 1678 | a | 1697 | | 1716 | A |
| 1679 | b | 1698 | | 1717 | B |
| | | | | 1718 | C |
| | | | | 1719 | D |
| 1680 | c | 1699 | | | |
| 1681 | d | 1700 | | 1720 | E |
| 1682 | e | 1701 | | | |
| 1683 | f | Anne 1702 | | | |
| 1684 | g | 1703 | | 1721 | F |
| Jas. II. 1685 | h | 1704 | | 1722 | G |
| 1686 | i | 1705 | | 1723 | H |
| 1687 | k | 1706 | | | |
| 1688 | l | 1707 | | 1724 | I |
| Wm. & My. 1689 | m | 1708 | | 1725 | K |
| 1690 | n | 1709 | | | |
| 1691 | o | 1710 | | | |
| 1692 | p | 1711 | | | |
| 1693 | q | 1712 | | | |
| 1694 | r | 1713 | | | |
| Wm. III. 1695 | s | Geo. I. 1714 | | | |
| 1696 to Mar. 27 1697 | t | 1715 | | | |

Although the use of the Britannia Standard was not compulsory after 30th May, 1720, it is still an authorised alternative standard and the marks are sometimes found in conjunction with date letters between 1720 and the present day.

e.g. 1721

22

# LONDON

| Date | Letter | Date | Letter | Date | Letter |
|------|--------|------|--------|------|--------|
| 1726 Geo II. | L | 1736 | a | 1756 | A |
| 1727 | M | 1737 | b | 1757 | B |
| 1728 | N | 1738 | C | 1758 | C |
| 1729 | O | 1739 | d | 1759 Geo. III. | D |
| 1730 | P | 1739 | d | 1760 | E |
| 1731 | Q | 1740 | e | 1761 | F |
| 1732 | R | 1741 | f | 1762 | G |
| 1733 | S | 1742 | g | 1763 | H |
| 1734 | T | 1743 | h | 1764 | I |
| 1735 | V | 1744 | i | 1765 | K |
| | | 1745 | k | 1766 | L |
| | | 1746 | l | 1767 | M |
| | | 1747 | m | 1768 | N |
| | | 1748 | n | 1769 | O |
| | | 1749 | o | 1770 | P |
| | | 1750 | p | 1771 | Q |
| | | 1751 | q | 1772 | R |
| | | 1752 | r | 1773 | S |
| | | 1753 | s | 1774 | T |
| | | 1754 | t | 1775 | U |
| | | 1755 | u | | |

This shield is also found occasionally between the years 1716 and 1728.

Numerous variations of the Leopard's Head and Lion passant occur between 1719 & 1729.

23

# LONDON

| | | | | | | | | |
|---|---|---|---|---|---|---|---|---|
| 1776 | **a** | | 1796 | **A** | ,, | 1816 | **a** | ,, |
| 1777 | **b** | | 1797 | **B** | ,, | 1817 | **b** | ,, |
| 1778 | **c** | | 1798 | **C** | ,, | 1818 | **c** | ,, |
| 1779 | **d** | | 1799 | **D** | ,, | 1819 | **d** | ,, |
| 1780 | **e** | | 1800 | **E** | ,, | Geo. IV 1820 | **e** | ,, |
| 1781 | **f** | | 1801 | **F** | ,, | | | |
| 1782 | **g** | | 1802 | **G** | ,, | 1821 | **f** | ,, |
| 1783 | **h** | | 1803 | **H** | ,, | 1822 | **g** | ,, |
| 1784 | **i** | | 1804 | **I** | ,, | 1823 | **h** | ,, |
| 1785 | **k** | ,, | 1805 | **K** | ,, | 1824 | **i** | ,, |
| 1786 | **l** | | 1806 | **L** | ,, | 1825 | **k** | ,, |
| 1787 | **m** | ,, | 1807 | **M** | ,, | 1826 | **l** | ,, |
| 1788 | **n** | ,, | 1808 | **N** | ,, | 1827 | **m** | ,, |
| 1789 | **o** | ,, | 1809 | **O** | ,, | 1828 | **n** | ,, |
| 1790 | **p** | ,, | 1810 | **P** | ,, | 1829 | **o** | ,, |
| 1791 | **q** | ,, | 1811 | **Q** | ,, | Wm. IV. 1830 | **p** | ,, |
| 1792 | **r** | ,, | 1812 | **R** | ,, | 1831 | **q** | |
| 1793 | **s** | ,, | 1813 | **S** | ,, | 1832 | **r** | ,, |
| 1794 | **t** | ,, | 1814 | **T** | ,, | 1833 | **s** | ,, |
| 1795 | **u** | ,, | 1815 | **U** | ,, | 1834 | **t** | |
| | | | | | | 1835 | **u** | ,, |

This shield, without point, is also found between the years 1776 and 1875, usually on small articles.

24

# LONDON

| | | | | | | | | |
|---|---|---|---|---|---|---|---|---|
| 1836 Vict. | A | ,, | 1856 | a | ,, | 1876 | AA | ,, |
| 1837 | B | ,, | 1857 | b | ,, | 1877 | B | ,, |
| 1838 | C | 😊 | 1858 | c | ,, | 1878 | C | ,, |
| 1839 | D | ,, | 1859 | d | ,, | 1879 | D | ,, |
| 1840 | E | ,, | 1860 | e | ,, | 1880 | E | ,, |
| 1841 | f | ,, | 1861 | f | ,, | 1881 | F | ,, |
| 1842 | G | ,, | 1862 | g | ,, | 1882 | G | ,, |
| 1843 | H | ,, | 1863 | h | ,, | 1883 | H | ,, |
| 1844 | J | ,, | 1864 | i | ,, | 1884 | I | ,, |
| 1845 | K | ,, | 1865 | k | ,, | 1885 | K | ,, |
| 1846 | L | ,, | 1866 | l | ,, | 1886 | L | ,, |
| 1847 | M | ,, | 1867 | m | ,, | 1887 | M | ,, |
| 1848 | N | ,, | 1868 | n | ,, | 1888 | N | ,, |
| 1849 | O | ,, | 1869 | o | ,, | 1889 | O | ,, |
| 1850 | P | ,, | 1870 | p | ,, | 1890 | P | ,, |
| 1851 | Q | ,, | 1871 | q | ,, | 1891 | Q | |
| 1852 | R | ,, | 1872 | r | ,, | 1892 | R | |
| 1853 | S | ,, | 1873 | s | ,, | 1893 | S | |
| 1854 | T | ,, | 1874 | t | ,, | 1894 | T | |
| 1855 | U | ,, | 1875 | u | ,, | 1895 | U | |

This shield, without point, is also found between the years 1776 and 1875, usually on small articles.

Queen's Head not used after 1890

25

# LONDON

| Year | Mark | Year | Mark | Year | Mark |
|------|------|------|------|------|------|
| 1896 | a | 1916 | a | Edw. VIII 1936 | A |
| 1897 | b | 1917 | b | Geo. VI 1937 | B |
| 1898 | c | 1918 | c | 1938 | C |
| 1899 | d | 1919 | d | 1939 | D |
| 1900 | e | 1920 | e | 1940 | E |
| Edw. VII 1901 | f | 1921 | f | 1941 | F |
| 1902 | g | 1922 | g | 1942 | G |
| 1903 | h | 1923 | h | 1943 | H |
| 1904 | i | 1924 | i | 1944 | I |
| 1905 | k | 1925 | k | 1945 | K |
| 1906 | l | 1926 | l | 1946 | L |
| 1907 | m | 1927 | m | 1947 | M |
| 1908 | n | 1928 | n | 1948 | N |
| 1909 Geo V 1910 | o | 1929 | o | 1949 | O |
| 1911 | p | 1930 | p | 1950 | P |
| 1912 | q | 1931 | q | 1951 | Q |
| 1913 | r | 1932 | r | Eliz. II 1952 | R |
| 1914 | s | 1933 | s | 1953 | S |
| 1915 | t | 1934 | t | 1954 | T |
| Britannia Standard Marks for 1927. | u m | 1935 | u | 1955 | U |

26

| | | | |
|---|---|---|---|
| 🦁 | 🐆 | | |
| 1956 | **a** | | |
| 1957 | **b** | | |
| 1958 | **c** | | |
| 1959 | **d** | | |
| 1960 | **e** | | |
| 1961 | **f** | | |
| 1962 | **g** | | |
| 1963 | **h** | | |

# BIRMINGHAM

| 1773 | A |   |
|------|---|---|
| 1774 | B |   |
| 1775 | C |   |
| 1776 | D |   |
| 1777 | E |   |
| 1778 | F |   |
| 1779 | G |   |
| 1780 | H |   |
| 1781 | I |   |
| 1782 | K |   |
| 1783 | L |   |
| 1784 | M |   |
| 1785 | N | ,, |
| 1786 | O |   |
| 1787 | P | ,, |
| 1788 | Q | ,, |
| 1789 | R | . |
| 1790 | S | ,, |
| 1791 | T | ,, |
| 1792 | U | ,, |
| 1793 | V | ,, |
| 1794 | W | ,, |
| 1795 | X | ,, |
| 1796 | Y | ,, |
| 1797 | Z | ,, |

| 1798 | a | ,, |
|------|---|---|
| 1799 | b | ,, |
| 1800 | c | ,, |
| 1801 | d | ,, |
| 1802 | e | ,, |
| 1803 | f | ,, |
| 1804 | g | ,, |
| 1805 | h | ,, |
| 1806 | i | ,, |
| 1807 | j | ,, |
| 1808 | k | ,, |
| 1809 | l |   |
| 1810 | m | ,, |
| 1811 | n | ,, |
| 1812 | o | ,, |
| 1813 | p | ,, |
| 1814 | q | ,, |
| 1815 | r | ,, |
| 1816 | s | ,, |
| 1817 | t | ,, |
| 1818 | u | ,, |
| 1819 | v | ,, |
| Geo. IV. 1820 | w | ,, |
| 1821 | x | ,, |
| 1822 | y | ,, |
| 1823 | z | ,, |

| 1824 | A | ,, |
|------|---|---|
| 1825 | B | ,, |
| 1826 | C | ,, |
| 1827 | D | ,, |
| 1828 | E | ,, |
| Wm. IV. 1829 | F | ,, |
| 1830 | G | ,, |
| 1831 | H |   |
| 1832 | J | ,, |
| 1833 | K | ,, |
| 1834 | L | ,, |
| 1835 | M |   |
| 1836 | N |   |
| Vict. 1837 | D | ,, |
| 1838 | P |   |
| 1839 | Q | ,, |
| 1840 | R |   |
| 1841 | S |   |
| 1842 | T |   |
| 1843 | U | ,, |
| 1844 | U | ,, |
| 1845 | W |   |
| 1846 | X | ,, |
| 1847 | Y | ,, |
| 1848 | Z | ,, |

In 1797 the duty on silver was doubled, and for a short time the King's Head was duplicated

# BIRMINGHAM

| 🦁⚓👑 | 🦁⚓👑 | 🦁⚓👑 |
|---|---|---|
| 1849 **A** ,, | 1867 **S** ,, | 1883 **i** ,, |
| 1850 **B** ,, | 1868 **T** ,, | 1884 **k** ,, |
| 1851 **C** ,, | 1869 **U** ,, | 1885 **l** ,, |
| 1852 **D** ,, | 1870 **V** ,, | 1886 **m** ,, |
| 1853 **E** ,, | 1871 **W** ,, | 1887 **n** ,, |
| 1854 **F** ,, | 1872 **X** ,, | 1888 **o** ,, |
| 1855 **G** ,, | 1873 **Y** ,, | 1889 **p** ,, |
| 1856 **H** ,, | 1874 **Z** ,, | 1890 **q** ,, |
| 1857 **I** ,, | | 1891 **r** |
| 1858 **J** ,, | 🦁⚓👑 | 1892 **s** |
| 1859 **K** ,, | 1875 **a** ,, | 1893 **t** |
| 1860 **L** ,, | 1876 **b** ,, | 1894 **u** |
| 1861 **M** ,, | 1877 **c** ,, | 1895 **v** |
| 1862 **N** ,, | 1878 **d** ,, | 1896 **m** |
| 1863 **O** ,, | 1879 **e** ,, | 1897 **x** |
| 1864 **P** ,, | 1880 **f** ,, | 1898 **y** |
| 1865 **Q** ,, | 1881 **g** ,, | 1899 **z** |
| 1866 **R** ,, | 1882 **h** ,, | |

# BIRMINGHAM

| | | | | | |
|---|---|---|---|---|---|
| 1900 | **a** | 1918 | **t** | 1933 | **J** |
| Edw. VII 1901 | **b** | 1919 | **u** | 1934 | **K** |
| 1902 | **c** | 1920 | **v** | 1935 | **L** |
| 1903 | **d** | 1921 | **w** | Edw. VIII 1936 | **M** |
| 1904 | **e** | 1922 | **x** | Geo. VI 1937 | **N** |
| 1905 | **f** | 1923 | **y** | 1938 | **O** |
| 1906 | **g** | 1924 | **z** | 1939 | **P** |
| 1907 | **h** | | | 1940 | **Q** |
| 1908 | **i** | | | 1941 | **R** |
| 1909 | **k** | 1925 | **A** | 1942 | **S** |
| Geo. V 1910 | **l** | 1926 | **B** | 1943 | **T** |
| 1911 | **m** | 1927 | **C** | 1944 | **U** |
| 1912 | **n** | 1928 | **D** | 1945 | **V** |
| 1913 | **o** | 1929 | **E** | 1946 | **W** |
| 1914 | **p** | 1930 | **F** | 1947 | **X** |
| 1915 | **q** | 1931 | **G** | 1948 | **Y** |
| 1916 | **r** | 1932 | **H** | 1949 | **Z** |
| 1917 | **s** | | | | |

# BIRMINGHAM

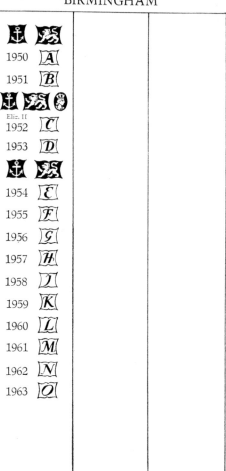

| | |
|---|---|
| 1950 | A |
| 1951 | B |
| Eliz. II 1952 | C |
| 1953 | D |
| 1954 | E |
| 1955 | F |
| 1956 | G |
| 1957 | H |
| 1958 | I |
| 1959 | K |
| 1960 | L |
| 1961 | M |
| 1962 | N |
| 1963 | O |

# CHESTER

| | | | | | |
|---|---|---|---|---|---|
| 1680 | | | 1701 Anne | A | 1726 Geo. II | A |
| | | | 1702 | B | 1727 | B |
| 1690 | | | 1703 | C | 1728 | C |
| | | | 1704 | D | 1729 | D |
| | | | 1705 | E | 1730 | E |
| 1690 to 1700 | STERLING | | 1706 | F | 1731 | F |
| | | | 1707 | G | 1732 | G |
| | | | 1708 | H | 1733 | K |
| | | | 1709 | I | 1734 | J |
| | | | 1710 | K | 1735 | K |
| | | | 1711 | L | 1736 | L |
| | | | 1712 | M | 1737 | M |
| | | | 1713 Geo. I 1714 | N O | 1738 | N |
| | | | 1715 | P | 1739 | O |
| | | | 1716 | Q | 1740 | P |
| | | | 1717 | R | 1741 | Q |
| | | | 1718 | S | 1742 | R |
| | | | | | 1743 | S |
| | | | | | 1744 | T |
| | | | 1719 | T | 1745 | U |
| | | | 1720 | U | 1746 | V |
| | | | 1721 | V | 1747 | W |
| | | | 1722 | W | 1748 | X |
| | | | 1723 | X | 1749 | Y or Y |
| | | | 1724 | Y | 1750 | Z |
| | | | 1725 | Z | | |

32

# CHESTER

| 🦁🏛️🛡️ | | | 🦁🏛️🛡️ | | | 🦁👑🛡️👤 | | |
|---|---|---|---|---|---|---|---|---|
| 1751 | **a** | | 1776 | **a** | | 1797 | **A** | „ |
| 1752 | **b** | | 1777 | **b** | | 1798 | **B** | „ |
| 1753 | **c** | | 1778 | **c** | | 1799 | **C** | „ |
| 1754 | **d** | | | | | | | |
| 1755 | **e** | | 🦁👑🛡️ | | | 🦁👑🛡️👤 | | |
| 1756 | **f** | | 1779 | **d** | | 1800 | **D** | „ |
| 1757 | **G** | | 1780 | **e** | | 1801 | **E** | „ |
| 1758 | **h** | | 1781 | **f** | | 1802 | **F** | „ |
| 1759 Geo. III | **i** | | 1782 | **g** | | 1803 | **G** | „ |
| 1760 | **k** | | 1783 | **h** | | 1804 | **H** | „ |
| 1761 | **l** | | | | | 1805 | **I** | |
| 1762 | **m** | | 🦁👑🛡️👤 | | | 1806 | **K** | „ |
| 1763 | **n** | | 1784 | **i** | „ | 1807 | **L** | „ |
| 1764 | **o** | | 1785 | **k** | „ | 1808 | **M** | „ |
| 1765 | **P** | | 1786 | **l** | 👤 | 1809 | **N** | „ |
| 1766 | **Q** | | 1787 | **m** | „ | 1810 | **O** | „ |
| 1767 | **R** | | 1788 | **n** | „ | 1811 | **P** | „ |
| 1768 | **S** | | 1789 | **o** | „ | 1812 | **Q** | „ |
| 1769 | **T** | | 1790 | **p** | „ | 1813 | **R** | „ |
| 1770 | **T** | | 1791 | **q** | „ | 1814 | **S** | „ |
| 1771 | **U** | | 1792 | **r** | „ | 1815 | **T** | „ |
| 1772 | **V** | | 1793 | **s** | „ | 1816 | **U** | „ |
| 1773 | **W** | | 1794 | **t** | „ | 1817 | **V** | „ |
| 1774 | **X** | | 1795 | **u** | „ | | | |
| 1775 | **Y** | | 1796 | **V** | „ | | | |

| 1818 Ⓐ ,, | 1839 Ⓐ ,, | 1864 Ⓐ ,, |
|---|---|---|
| 1819 Ⓑ ,, | 1840 Ⓑ ,, | 1865 Ⓑ ,, |
| Geo IV | 1841 Ⓒ ,, | 1866 Ⓒ ,, |
| 1820 Ⓒ ,, | 1842 Ⓓ ,, | 1867 Ⓓ ,, |
| 1821 Ⓓ ,, | 1843 Ⓔ ,, | 1868 Ⓔ ,, |
| 1822 Ⓓ ,, | 1844 Ⓕ ,, | 1869 Ⓕ ,, |
| | 1845 Ⓖ ,, | 1870 Ⓖ ,, |
| 1823 Ⓔ ,, | 1846 Ⓗ ,, | 1871 Ⓗ ,, |
| 1824 Ⓕ ,, | 1847 Ⓙ ,, | 1872 Ⓘ ,, |
| 1825 Ⓖ ,, | 1848 Ⓚ ,, | 1873 Ⓚ ,, |
| 1826 Ⓗ ,, | 1849 Ⓛ ,, | 1874 Ⓛ ,, |
| 1827 Ⓘ ,, | 1850 Ⓜ ,, | 1875 Ⓜ ,, |
| 1828 Ⓚ ,, | 1851 Ⓝ ,, | 1876 Ⓝ ,, |
| 1829 Ⓛ ,, | 1852 Ⓞ ,, | 1877 Ⓞ ,, |
| Wm. IV. | 1853 Ⓟ ,, | 1878 Ⓟ ,, |
| 1830 Ⓜ ,, | 1854 Ⓠ ,, | 1879 Ⓠ ,, |
| 1831 Ⓝ ,, | 1855 Ⓡ ,, | 1880 Ⓡ ,, |
| 1832 Ⓞ ,, | 1856 Ⓢ ,, | 1881 Ⓢ ,, |
| 1833 Ⓟ ,, | 1857 Ⓣ ,, | 1882 Ⓣ ,, |
| 1834 Ⓠ ,, | 1858 Ⓤ ,, | 1883 Ⓤ ,, |
| 1835 Ⓡ | 1859 Ⓥ ,, | |
| 1836 Ⓢ ,, | 1860 Ⓦ ,, | |
| Vict. | 1861 Ⓧ ,, | |
| 1837 Ⓣ ,, | 1862 Ⓨ ,, | |
| 1838 Ⓤ ,, | 1863 Ⓩ ,, | |

# CHESTER

| 1884 | A | Edw. VII 1901 | A | 1926 | a |
|------|---|------|---|------|---|
| 1885 | B | 1902 | B | 1927 | b |
| 1886 | C | 1903 | C | 1928 | c |
| 1887 | D | 1904 | D | 1929 | d |
| 1888 | E | 1905 | E | 1930 | e |
| 1889 | F | 1906 | F | 1931 | ff |
| | | 1907 | G | 1932 | G |
| 1890 | G | 1908 | H | | |
| 1891 | H | 1909 | I | 1933 | h |
| 1892 | I | Geo. V 1910 | K | 1934 | j |
| 1893 | K | 1911 | L | 1935 | k |
| 1894 | L | 1912 | M | | |
| 1895 | M | 1913 | N | Edw. VIII 1936 | l |
| 1896 | N | 1914 | O | Geo. VI 1937 | m |
| 1897 | O | 1915 | P | 1938 | n |
| 1898 | P | 1916 | Q | 1939 | o |
| 1899 | Q | 1917 | R | 1940 | p |
| 1900 | R | 1918 | S | 1941 | q |
| | | 1919 | T | 1942 | r |
| | | 1920 | U | 1943 | s |
| | | 1921 | V | 1944 | t |
| | | 1922 | W | 1945 | u |
| | | 1923 | X | 1946 | v |
| | | 1924 | Y | 1947 | w |
| | | 1925 | Z | | |

Since 1839 both shields have been in use for the Sterling Mark and since 1900 for the Date Letter also.

| | |
|---|---|
| 🦁 🛡️ | |
| 1948 𝕏 | |
| 1949 Y | |
| 1950 Z | |
| 1951 A | |
| 🦁 🛡️ 👤 Eliz. II | |
| 1952 B | |
| 1953 C | |
| 🦁 🛡️ | |
| 1954 D | |
| 1955 E | |
| 1956 F | |
| 1957 G | |
| 1958 H | |
| 1959 J | |
| 1960 K | |
| 1961 L | |
| 1st July to 24 Aug. 1962 M | |

The Chester
Assay Office
closed 24th
August, 1962

# DUBLIN

| Year | Mark | Year | Mark | Year | Mark |
|---|---|---|---|---|---|
| Chas. I 1638 | A | 1658 | a | 1678 | A |
| 1639 | B | 1659 | b | 1679 | B |
| 1640 | C | Chas. II 1660 | c | 1680 | C |
| 1641 | D | 1661 | d | 1681 | D |
| 1642 | E | 1662 | e | 1682 | E |
| 1643 | F | 1663 | f | 1683-4 | F |
| 1644 | G | 1664 | g | Jas. II 1685-7 | G |
| 1645 | H | 1665 | h | 1688-93 | h |
| 1646 | I | 1666 | i | Wm. III 1694-5 | K |
| 1647 | K | 1667 | k | 1696-8 | L |
| 1648 | L | 1668 | l | 1699 | M |
| Com'w'th 1649 | M | 1669 | m | 1700 | N |
| 1650 | N | 1670 | n | 1701 | O |
| 1651 | O | 1671 | O | Anne 1702 | P |
| 1652 | P | 1672 | p | 1703 | Q |
| 1653 | Q | 1673 | q | 1704-5 | R |
| 1654 | R | 1674 | r | 1706-7 | S |
| 1655 | S | 1675 | s | 1708-9 | T |
| 1656 | T | 1676 | t | 1710-11 | U |
| 1657 | U | 1677 | u | 1712-13 | W |
| | | | | Geo. I 1714 | X |
| | | | | 1715 | Y |
| | | | | 1716 | Z |

# DUBLIN

| 1717 | a |
| 1718 | B |
| 1719 | C |

| 1720 | A |
| 1721 | B |
| 1722 | C |
| 1723 | D |
| 1724 | E |
| 1725 | F |
| 1726 | G |
| Geo. II 1727 | H |
| 1728 | I |
| 1729 | K |
| 1730 | L |

| 1731 | L |
| 1732 | M |
| 1733 | N |
| 1734 | O |
| 1735 | P |
| 1736 | Q |
| 1737 | R |
| 1738 | S |
| 1739 | T |
| 1740 | U U |
| 1741-2 | U W |
| 1743-4 | X |
| 1745 | Y |
| 1746 | Z |

Alternative
Harp crowned
c.1739-1748.

| 1747 | A |
| 1748 | B |
| 1749 | C |
| 1750 | D |
| 1751 | E |
| 1752 | F |
| 1753 | G |
| 1754 | H |
| 1757 | I |
| 1758 | K |
| 1759 | L |
| Geo. III 1760 | M |
| 1761 | N |
| 1762 | O |
| 1763 | P |
| 1764 | Q |
| 1765 | R |
| 1766 | S |
| 1767 | T |
| 1768 | U |
| 1769 | W |
| 1770 | X |
| 1771 | Y |
| 1772 | Z |

Alternative
Hibernia
1751-1752

# DUBLIN

| | | | | | |
|---|---|---|---|---|---|
| 1773 | Ⓐ | | 1797 | Ⓐ | |
| 1774 | Ⓑ | | 1798 | Ⓑ | |
| 1775 | Ⓒ | | 1799 | Ⓒ | |
| 1776 | Ⓓ | | 1800 | Ⓓ | |
| 1777 | Ⓔ | | 1801 | Ⓔ | |
| 1778 | Ⓕ | | 1802 | Ⓕ | |
| 1779 | Ⓖ | | 1803 | Ⓖ | |
| 1780 | Ⓗ | | 1804 | Ⓗ | |
| 1781 | Ⓘ | | 1805 | Ⓘ | |
| 1782 | Ⓚ | | 1806 | Ⓚ | |
| 1783 | Ⓛ | | 1807 | Ⓛ | ☺ |
| 1784 | Ⓜ | | 1808 | Ⓜ | ,, |
| 1785 | Ⓝ | | 1809 | Ⓝ | |
| 1786 | Ⓞ | | 1810 | Ⓞ | ,, |
| 1787 | Ⓟ | | 1811 | Ⓟ | ,, |
| 1788 | Ⓠ | | 1812 | Ⓠ | ,, |
| 1789 | Ⓡ | | 1813 | Ⓡ | ,, |
| 1790 | Ⓢ | | 1814 | Ⓢ | ,, |
| 1791 | Ⓣ | | 1815 | Ⓣ | ,, |
| 1792 | Ⓤ | | 1816 | Ⓤ | ,, |
| 1793 | Ⓦ | | 1817 | Ⓦ | ,, |
| 1794 | Ⓧ | | 1818 | Ⓧ | ,, |
| 1795 | Ⓨ | | 1819 Geo. IV | Ⓨ | ,, |
| 1796 | Ⓩ | | 1820 | Ⓩ | ,, |

Throughout this cycle the shape of the shield varies considerably.

| | | | | | | | | |
|---|---|---|---|---|---|---|---|---|
| 1821 | A | | | Vict. 1837 | R | | |
| 1822 | " B | " | | 1838 | " S | " | |
| 1823 | " C | " | " | 1839 | " T | | " |
| 1824 | " D | " | " | 1840 | " U | " | " |
| 1825 | " E e | " | " | 1841 | " V | " | " |
| 1826 | " F | " | " | 1842 | W | | |
| 1827 | G | | | 1843 | " X | " | " |
| 1828 | H | | | 1844 | Y | | " |
| 1829 | I | | | 1845 | Z | | " |
| Wm. IV 1830 | K | | | 1846 | a | | |
| 1831 | L | | | 1847 | " b | " | " |
| 1832 | " M | " | " | 1848 | " c | " | " |
| 1833 | N | | | 1849 | " d | " | " |
| 1834 | O | | | 1850 | " e | " | " |
| 1835 | " P | " | " | 1851 | " f f | " | " |
| 1836 | " Q | " | " | 1852 | " g g | " | " |
| | | | | 1853 | " h h | " | " |
| | | | | 1854 | " j | " | " |

# DUBLIN

| | | | | | |
|---|---|---|---|---|---|
| 1855 | k | " | 1871 | A | " |
| 1856 | l | " | 1872 | B | .. |
| | | | 1873 | C | " |
| 1857 | m | " | 1874 | D | " |
| 1858 | n | " | 1875 | E | " |
| | | | 1876 | F | " |
| 1859 | O | " | 1877 | G | " |
| 1860 | P | " | 1878 | H | " |
| | | | 1879 | I | " |
| 1861 | Q | " | 1880 | K | " |
| | | | 1881 | L | " |
| 1862 | r | " | 1882 | M | " |
| 1863 | S | " | 1883 | N | " |
| | | | 1884 | O | " |
| 1864 | t | " | 1885 | P | " |
| | | | 1886 | Q | " |
| 1865 | u | " | 1887 | R | " |
| 1866 | V | " | 1888 | S | " |
| | | | 1889 | T | " |
| 1867 | W | " | 1890 | U | " |
| 1868 | X | " | 1891 | V | |
| | | | 1892 | W | |
| 1869 | Y | " | 1893 | X | |
| 1870 | Z | " | 1894 | Y | |
| | | | 1895 | Z | |

41

# DUBLIN

| | | | | | |
|---|---|---|---|---|---|
| 1896 | A | 1916 | A | 1937 | V |
| 1897 | B | 1917 | b | 1938 | W |
| 1898 | C | 1918 | C | 1939 | X |
| 1899 | D | 1919 | D | 1940 | Y |
| 1900 | E | 1920 | e | 1941 | Z |
| Edw. VII 1901 | F | 1921 | F | | |
| 1902 | G | 1922 | S | | |
| 1903 | H | 1923 | h | 1942 | A |
| 1904 | I | 1924 | i | 1943 | B |
| 1905 | K | 1925 | k | 1944 | C |
| 1906 | L | 1926 | l | 1945 | D |
| 1907 | M | 1927 | m | | |
| 1908 | N | 1928 | n | 1946 | E |
| 1909 | O | 1929 | o | 1947 | F |
| Geo. V 1910 | P | 1930-31 | p | 1948 | G |
| 1911 | Q | 1932 | Q | 1949 | H |
| 1912 | R | 1933 | R | 1950 | I |
| 1913 | S | 1934 | S | 1951 | J |
| 1914 | T | 1935 | T | 1952 | K |
| 1915 | U | 1936 | U | 1953 | L |
| | | | | 1954 | M |

Up to 1931 the date letter was changed on 1st June. The Q of 1932 began on 1st January.

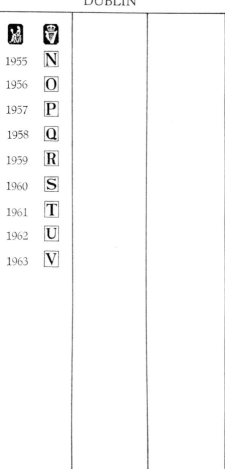

| | | | |
|---|---|---|---|
| 1955 | N | | |
| 1956 | O | | |
| 1957 | P | | |
| 1958 | Q | | |
| 1959 | R | | |
| 1960 | S | | |
| 1961 | T | | |
| 1962 | U | | |
| 1963 | V | | |

| TOWN MARK | DEACON'S MARK | | TOWN MARK | DEACON'S MARK | | | |
|---|---|---|---|---|---|---|---|
| 1552 | | | 1616-35 | | | 1681 | a |
| 1563 | " | IC | 1633 | | | | B |
| c.1570 | " | | 1637 | | IS | 1682 | b |
| 1576 | | | 1640 | | T | 1683 | c |
| 1585 | " | M | 1642 | " | IF | 1684 | d |
| 1590 | | | 1643 | | | 1685 | e |
| 1591 | " | | 1644 | " | A | 1686 | f |
| 1591-4 | " | | 1649 | " | GC | 1687 | g |
| 1596 | | EK | 1651 | " | IF | 1688 Wm. & Mary 1689 | h i |
| 1609 | " | R | 1660 | " | YB | 1690 1691 1692 | k l m |
| 1611 | | D | 1665 | " | IS | 1693 | n |
| 1617 | | IL | 1669 | " | AR | 1694 Wm. III. 1695 | o p |
| c.1617 | " | G | 1663-81 | " | E | 1696 | q |
| 1613-21 | | | 1675 | " | | 1697 | r |

# EDINBURGH

| | | | | | |
|---|---|---|---|---|---|
| 🏰 | 𝓟 | 🏰 | **EP** | 🏰 | **AU** |
| 1698 | §̣ | Geo I. 1714 | **K** | 1730 | Ⓐ |
| 1699 | t̃ | 1715 | **L** | 1731 | Ⓑ |
| 1700 | ũ | 1716 | **M** | 1732 | Ⓒ |
| 1701 | ũ̃ | 1717 | **N** | 1733 | Ⓓ |
| Anne 1702 | 🏰 ĩ | 🏰 | **EP** | 1734 | Ⓔ |
| 1703 | ỹ | 1718 | **O** | 1735 | Ⓕ |
| 1704 | ȷ̃ | 1719 | **P P** | 1736 | Ⓖ |
| | | 🏰 | **EP** | 1737 | Ⓗ |
| 🏰 | 𝓟 | 1720 | **q** | 1738 | Ⓘ |
| 1705 | **A** | 1721 | **R** | 1739 | Ⓚ |
| 1706 | **B** | 1722 | **S** | 🏰 | **GED** |
| 🏰 | **EP** | 1723 | **T** | 1740 | Ⓛ |
| 1707 | **C** | 1724 | **u** | 1741 | 𝓜 |
| 1708 | **D** | 1725 | **V V** | 🏰 | **EL** |
| 1709 | **E** | 1726 Geo. II 1727 | **W** **X** | 1742 | 𝒩 |
| 1710 | **F** | 1728 | **Y** | 1743 | O |
| 1711 | **G** | 1729 | **Z** | 🏰 | **HG** |
| 🏰 | **EP** | | | 1744 | 𝓟 |
| 1712 | **H** | | | 1745 | Ⓠ |
| 1713 | **I** | | | 1746 | Ⓡ |

45

# EDINBURGH

| 1747 | S |
|------|---|
| 1748 | T |
| 1749 | U |
| 1750 | U |
| 1751 | W |
| 1752 | X |
| 1753 | Y |
| 1754 | Z |

| 1755 | A |
|------|---|
| 1756 | B |
| 1757 | C |
| 1758 | D |

| 1759 | E |
|------|---|
| Geo III. 1760 | F |
| 1761 | G |
| 1762 | H |

| 1763 | I J |
|------|-----|
| 1764 | K |
| 1765 | L |
| 1766 | M |
| 1767 | N |
| 1768 | O |
| 1769 | P |
| 1770 | Q |
| 1771 | R |
| 1772 | S |
| 1773 | T |
| 1774 | U |
| 1775 | V |
| 1776 | W |
| 1777 | Y |
| 1778 | Z |
| 1779 | U |

| 1780 | A |  |
|------|---|--|
| 1781 | B |  |
| 1782 | C |  |
| 1783 | D |  |
| 1784 | E |  |
| 1785 | F | ,, |
| 1786 | G |  |
| 1787 | ,, | ,, |
| 1788 | H | ,, |
| 1789 | I J | ,, |
| 1790 | K | ,, |
| 1791 | L | ,, |
| 1792 | M | ,, |
| 1793 | N N | ,, |
| 1794 | O O | ,, |
| 1795 | P | ,, |
| 1796 | Q | ,, |

Alternative Town Marks about 1771.

46

| Year | Letter | Mark | Year | Letter | Mark | Year | Letter | Mark |
|------|--------|------|------|--------|------|------|--------|------|
| 1797 | R R | | 1813 | h | " | 1832 | A | |
| 1798 | S | " | 1814 | i | " | 1833 | B | " |
| | | | 1815 | j | " | 1834 | C | " |
| 1799 | T | | 1816 | k | " | 1835 | D | " |
| 1800 | U | " | 1817 | l | " | 1836 | E | " |
| 1801 | V | " | 1818 | m | " | Vict. | | |
| | | | 1819 | n | " | 1837 | f | " |
| 1802 | W | | | | | 1838 | G | " |
| 1803 | X | " | Geo IV | | | 1839 | H | " |
| 1804 | Y | " | 1820 | o | | 1840 | J | " |
| 1805 | Z | " | 1821 | p | " | 1841 | K | |
| | | | 1822 | q | " | 1842 | L | " |
| | | | 1823 | r | " | 1843 | m | " |
| 1806 | a | | | | | 1844 | N | " |
| 1807 | b | " | 1824 | S | | 1845 | O | " |
| 1808 | c | " | 1825 | t | " | 1846 | P | " |
| | | | | | | 1847 | Q | " |
| 1809 | d | | 1826 | u | | 1848 | R | " |
| 1810 | e | " | 1827 | V | " | 1849 | S | " |
| 1811 | f | " | 1828 | W | " | 1850 | T | " |
| 1812 | g | " | 1829 | X | " | 1851 | U | " |
| | | | Wm IV | | | 1852 | V | " |
| | | | 1830 | y | " | 1853 | W | " |
| | | | 1831 | z | " | 1854 | X | ' |
| | | | | | | 1855 | Y | " |
| | | | | | | 1856 | Z | " |

# EDINBURGH

| | | | | | | | | |
|---|---|---|---|---|---|---|---|---|
| 1857 | (A) | 1875 | (T) | 1890 | (i) |
| 1858 | (B) | 1876 | (U) | 1891 | (k) |
| 1859 | (C) | 1877 | (V) | 1892 | (l) |
| 1860 | (D) | 1878 | (W) | 1893 | (m) |
| 1861 | (E) | 1879 | (X) | 1894 | (n) |
| 1862 | (F) | 1880 | (Y) | 1895 | (o) |
| 1863 | (G) | 1881 | (Z) | 1896 | (p) |
| 1864 | (H) | | | 1897 | (q) |
| 1865 | (I) | | | 1898 | (r) |
| 1866 | (K) | | | 1899 | (s) |
| 1867 | (L) | 1882 | (a) | 1900 | (t) |
| 1868 | (M) | 1883 | (b) | Edw.VII 1901 | (v) |
| 1869 | (N) | 1884 | (c) | 1902 | (w) |
| 1870 | (O) | 1885 | (d) | 1903 | (x) |
| 1871 | (P) | 1886 | (e) | 1904 | (y) |
| 1872 | (Q) | 1887 | (f) | 1905 | (z) |
| 1873 | (R) | 1888 | (g) | | |
| 1874 | (S) | 1889 | (h) | | |

# EDINBURGH

| | | | | | |
|---|---|---|---|---|---|
| 1906 | Ⓐ | 1924 | Ⓣ | 1939 | Ⓙ |
| 1907 | Ⓑ | 1925 | Ⓤ | 1940 | Ⓚ |
| 1908 | Ⓒ | 1926 | Ⓥ | 1941 | Ⓛ |
| 1909 | Ⓓ | 1927 | Ⓦ | 1942 | Ⓜ |
| Geo.V 1910 | Ⓔ | 1928 | Ⓧ | 1943 | Ⓝ |
| 1911 | Ⓕ | 1929 | Ⓨ | 1944 | Ⓞ |
| 1912 | Ⓖ | 1930 | Ⓩ | 1945 | Ⓟ |
| 1913 | Ⓗ | | | 1946 | Ⓠ |
| 1914 | Ⓘ | 1931 | Ⓐ | 1947 | Ⓡ |
| 1915 | Ⓚ | 1932 | Ⓑ | 1948 | Ⓢ |
| 1916 | Ⓛ | 1933 | Ⓒ | 1949 | Ⓣ |
| 1917 | Ⓜ | 1934 | Ⓓ | 1950 | Ⓤ |
| 1918 | Ⓝ | 1935 | Ⓔ | 1951 | Ⓥ |
| 1919 | Ⓞ | Edw.VIII 1936 | Ⓕ | Eliz. II 1952 | Ⓦ |
| 1920 | Ⓟ | Geo VI 1937 | Ⓖ | 1953 | Ⓧ |
| 1921 | Ⓠ | 1938 | Ⓗ | 1954 | Ⓨ |
| 1922 | Ⓡ | | | 1955 | Ⓩ |
| 1923 | Ⓢ | | | | |

| | | | |
|---|---|---|---|
| 徽 | 🌿 | | |
| 1956 | 𝔄 | | |
| 1957 | 𝔅 | | |
| 1958 | ℭ | | |
| 1959 | 𝔇 | | |
| 1960 | 𝔈 | | |
| 1961 | 𝔉 | | |
| 1962 | 𝔊 | | |
| 1963 | ℌ | | |

| | | |
|---|---|---|
| c. 1570 | | |
| c. 1571 | | |
| c. 1575 | | |
| c. 1580 | | |
| c. 1585 | | |
| to | | |
| c. 1630 various | | |
| c. 1635 | | |
| to | | |
| c. 1675 | | |
| variations of both | | |
| c. 1680 | | |
| c. 1690 | | |
| c. 1698 | | |

| Year | Letter |
|---|---|
| 1701 | A |
| Anne 1702 | B |
| 1703 | C |
| 1704 | D |
| 1705 | E |
| 1706 | F |
| 1707 | G |
| 1708 | H |
| 1709 | I |
| 1710 | K |
| 1711 | L |
| 1712 | M |
| 1713 | N |
| Geo. I 1714 | O |
| 1715 | P |
| 1716 | Q |
| 1717 | R |
| 1718 | S |
| 1719 | T |
| 1720 | V |
| 1721 | W |
| 1722 | X |
| 1723 | Y |
| 1724 | Z |

51

# EXETER

| 1725 | a | 1749 | A | 1773 | A |
| 1726 | b | 1750 | B | 1774 | B |
| Geo. II | | 1751 | C | 1775 | C |
| 1727 | c | 1752 | D | 1776 | D |
| 1728 | d | 1753 | E | 1777 | E |
| 1729 | e | 1754 | F | 1778 | F |
| 1730 | f | 1755 | G | 1779 | G |
| 1731 | g | 1756 | H | 1780 | H |
| 1732 | h | 1757 | I | 1781-2 | I |
| 1733 | i | 1758 | K | 1783 | K |
| 1734 | k | 1759 | L | 1784 | L |
| 1735 | l | Geo. III | | 1785 | M |
| 1736 | m | 1760 | M | 1786 | N |
| 1737 | n | 1761 | N | 1787 | O |
| 1738 | o | 1762 | O | 1788 | P |
| 1739 | p | 1763 | P | 1789 | q |
| 1740 | q | 1764 | Q | 1790 | r |
| 1741 | r | 1765 | R | 1791 | f |
| 1742 | s | 1766 | S | 1792 | t |
| 1743 | t | 1767 | T | 1793 | u |
| 1744 | u | 1768 | U | 1794 | W |
| 1745 | w | 1769 | W | 1795 | X |
| 1746 | x | 1770 | X | 1796 | y |
| 1747 | y | 1771 | Y | | |
| 1748 | z | 1772 | Z | | |

Leopard's head
not used after
1777

52

# EXETER

| 1797 | A | " |
|------|---|---|
| 1798 | B | " |
| 1799 | C | 🖼 |
| 1800 | D | " |
| 1801 | E | " |
| 1802 | F | " |
| 1803 | G | " |
| 1804 | H | " |

| 1805 | I | " |
|------|---|---|
| 1806 | K | " |
| 1807 | L | " |
| 1808 | M | " |
| 1809 | N | " |
| 1810 | O | " |
| 1811 | P | " |
| 1812 | Q | " |
| 1813 | R | " |
| 1814 | S | " |
| 1815 | T | " |
| 1816 | U | " |

| 1817 | a | " |
|------|---|---|
| 1818 | b | " |
| 1819 Geo. IV. | c | " |
| 1820 | d | " |
| 1821 | e | " |
| 1822 | f | 🖼 |
| 1823 | g | " |
| 1824 | h | " |
| 1825 | i | " |
| 1826 | k | " |
| 1827 | l | " |
| 1828 | m | " |
| 1829 Wm. IV. | n | " |
| 1830 | o | " |

| 1831 | p | " |
|------|---|---|
| 1832 | q | " |

| 1833 | r | " |
|------|---|---|
| 1834 | s | 🖼 |
| 1835 | t | " |
| 1836 | u | " |

| Vict. 1837 | A | 🖼 |
|------|---|---|
| 1838 | B | 🖼 |
| 1839 | C | " |
| 1840 | D | " |

| 1841 | E | " |
|------|---|---|
| 1842 | F | " |

| 1843 | G | " |
|------|---|---|
| 1844 | H | " |
| 1845 | J | " |
| 1846 | K | " |
| 1847 | L | " |
| 1848 | M | " |
| 1849 | A | " |
| 1850 | O | " |
| 1851 | P | " |
| 1852 | Q | " |
| 1853 | R | " |
| 1854 | S | " |
| 1855 | T | " |
| 1856 | U | " |

53

# EXETER

| 🏰 | 🦁 | 👤 | 🏰 | 🦁 | 👤 |
|---|---|---|---|---|---|
| 1857 | Ⓐ | " | 1877 | Ⓐ | " |
| 1858 | Ⓑ | " | 1878 | Ⓑ | " |
| 1859 | Ⓒ | " | 1879 | Ⓒ | " |
| 1860 | Ⓓ | " | 1880 | Ⓓ | " |
| 1861 | Ⓔ | " | 1881 | Ⓔ | " |
| 1862 | Ⓕ | " | 1882 | Ⓕ | " |
| 1863 | Ⓖ | " | | | |
| 1864 | Ⓗ | " | | | |
| 1865 | Ⓘ | " | | | |
| 1866 | Ⓚ | " | | | |
| 1867 | Ⓛ | " | | | |
| 1868 | Ⓜ | " | | | |
| 1869 | Ⓝ | " | | | |
| 1870 | Ⓞ | " | | | |
| 1871 | Ⓟ | " | | | |
| 1872 | Ⓠ | " | | | |
| 1873 | Ⓡ | " | | | |
| 1874 | Ⓢ | " | | | |
| 1875 | Ⓣ | " | | | |
| 1876 | Ⓤ | " | | | |

# GLASGOW

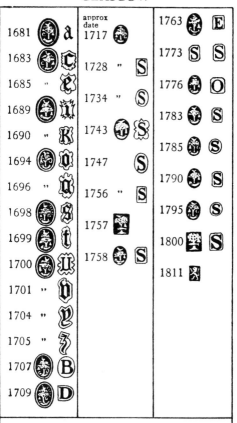

| | | approx date | | | |
|---|---|---|---|---|---|
| 1681 | | 1717 | | 1763 | E |
| 1683 | | 1728 " | S | 1773 | S | S |
| 1685 " | | 1734 " | S | 1776 | O |
| 1689 | | 1743 | S | 1783 | S |
| 1690 " | | 1747 | | 1785 | S |
| 1694 | | 1756 " | S | 1790 | S |
| 1696 " | | 1757 | | 1795 | S |
| 1698 | | 1758 | S | 1800 | S |
| 1699 | | | | 1811 | |
| 1700 | | | | | |
| 1701 " | | | | | |
| 1704 " | | | | | |
| 1705 " | | | | | |
| 1707 | B | | | | |
| 1709 | D | | | | |

The maker s mark was stamped in duplicate
on either side of the town mark up to the year
1800. From 1681-1710 a date letter was used
but was discontinued from 1710-1819. The
letter S probably signified Sterling

55

# GLASGOW

| Year | Mark | | Year | Mark | | Year | Mark | |
|------|------|---|------|------|---|------|------|---|
| 1819 | A | " | Vict. 1837 | S | " | 1853 | I | " |
| Geo. IV 1820 | B | " | 1838 | T | " | 1854 | J | " |
| 1821 | C | " | 1839 | U | " | 1855 | K | " |
| 1822 | D | " | 1840 | V | " | 1856 | L | " |
| 1823 | E | " | 1841 | W | | 1857 | M | " |
| 1824 | F | " | 1842 | X | " | 1858 | N | " |
| 1825 | G | " | 1843 | Y | " | 1859 | O | " |
| 1826 | H | " | 1844 | Z | " | 1860 | P | " |
| 1827 | I | " | | | | 1861 | Q | " |
| 1828 | J | " | 1845 | A | " | 1862 | R | " |
| 1829 | K | " | 1846 | B | " | 1863 | S | " |
| Wm. IV 1830 | L | " | 1847 | C | " | 1864 | T | " |
| 1831 | M | " | 1848 | D | " | 1865 | U | " |
| 1832 | N | | 1849 | E | " | 1866 | O | " |
| 1833 | O | " | 1850 | F | " | 1867 | W | " |
| 1834 | P | " | 1851 | G | " | 1868 | X | " |
| 1835 | Q | " | 1852 | K | " | 1869 | Y | " |
| 1836 | R | " | | | | 1870 | Z | " |

# GLASGOW

| | | | | | | | | |
|---|---|---|---|---|---|---|---|---|
| 1871 | Ⓐ | ,, | 1897 | 𝒜 | | 1914 | ℛ | |
| 1872 | Ⓑ | ,, | 1898 | ℬ | | 1915 | 𝒮 | |
| 1873 | Ⓒ | ,, | 1899 | 𝒞 | | 1916 | 𝒯 | |
| 1874 | Ⓓ | ,, | 1900 | 𝒟 | | 1917 | 𝒰 | |
| 1875 | Ⓔ | ,, | Edw. VII | | | 1918 | 𝒱 | |
| 1876 | Ⓕ | ,, | 1901 | ℰ | | 1919 | 𝒲 | |
| 1877 | Ⓖ | ,, | 1902 | ℱ | | 1920 | 𝒳 | |
| 1878 | Ⓗ | ,, | 1903 | 𝒢 | | 1921 | 𝒴 | |
| 1879 | Ⓘ | ,, | 1904 | ℋ | | 1922 | 𝒵 | |
| 1880 | Ⓙ | ,, | 1905 | 𝒥 | | | | |
| 1881 | Ⓚ | ,, | 1906 | 𝒦 | | | | |
| 1882 | Ⓛ | ,, | 1907 | 𝒦 | | 1923 | ⓐ | |
| 1883 | Ⓜ | ,, | 1908 | ℒ | | 1924 | ⓑ | |
| 1884 | Ⓝ | ,,, | 1909 | ℳ | | 1925 | ⓒ | |
| 1885 | Ⓞ | ,, | Geo. V | | | 1926 | ⓓ | |
| 1886 | Ⓟ | ,: | 1910 | 𝒩 | | 1927 | ⓔ | |
| 1887 | Ⓠ | ,, | 1911 | 𝒪 | | 1928 | ⓕ | |
| 1888 | Ⓡ | ,, | 1912 | 𝒫 | | 1929 | ⓖ | |
| 1889 | Ⓢ | ,, | 1913 | 𝒬 | | | | |
| 1890 | Ⓣ | ,, | | | | | | |
| 1891 | Ⓤ | | | | | | | |
| 1892 | Ⓥ | | | | | | | |
| 1893 | Ⓦ | | | | | | | |
| 1894 | Ⓧ | | | | | | | |
| 1895 | Ⓨ | | | | | | | |
| 1896 | Ⓩ | | | | | | | |

# GLASGOW

| | | |
|---|---|---|
| 1930 **h** | 1945 **W** | 1958 **l** |
| 1931 **i** | 1946 **X** | 1959 **m** |
| 1932 **j** | 1947 **y** | 1960 **n** |
| 1933 **k** | 1948 **Z** | 1961 **o** |
| 1934 **l** | | 1962 **p** |
| 1935 **m** | 1949 **a** | 1963 **R** |
| Edw. VIII 1936 **n** | 1950 **B** | 1st July, 1963 to 31st March, 1964 |
| Geo. VI 1937 **o** | 1951 **C** | The Glasgow Assay Office closed 31st March 1964 |
| 1938 **p** | Eliz. II 1952 **D** | |
| 1939 **q** | 1953 **e** | |
| 1940 **r** | 1954 **F** | |
| 1941 **s** | 1955 **J** | |
| 1942 **t** | 1956 **H** | |
| 1943 **u** | 1957 **I** | |
| 1944 **v** | | |

| | | |
|---|---|---|
| | (hallmark images) | (hallmark images) |
| c.1658 to c.1670 | Anne 1702 Ⓐ | 1721 Ⓐ |
| | 1703 Ⓑ | 1722 Ⓑ |
| | 1704 Ⓒ | 1723 Ⓒ |
| | 1705 | 1724 Ⓓ |
| c.1672 to c.1684 | 1706 Ⓔ | 1725 Ⓔ |
| | 1707 Ⓕ | 1726 Ⓕ |
| c.1685 to c.1694 | 1708 Ⓖ | Geo. II. 1727 Ⓖ |
| | 1709 | |
| c.1696 | 1710 | 1728 Ⓗ |
| | 1711 | 1729 Ⓘ |
| | 1712 Ⓗ | 1730 Ⓚ |
| | 1713 | 1731 Ⓛ |
| | | 1732 Ⓜ |
| c.1700 | | 1733 Ⓝ |
| | Geo. I. 1714 Ⓓ | 1734 Ⓞ |
| | 1715 | 1735 Ⓟ |
| | 1716 | 1736 Ⓠ |
| | 1717 Ⓟ | 1737 Ⓡ |
| | 1718 Ⓠ | 1738 Ⓢ |
| | 1719 Ⓓ | 1739 Ⓣ |
| | 1720 Ⓔ | Between 1721 and 1728, shapes of shields and lion passant vary, and lion sometimes faces left. |

# NEWCASTLE

| 1740 | A |
|------|---|
| 1741 | B |
| 1742 | C |
| 1743 | D |
| 1744 | E |
| 1745 | F |
| 1746 | G |
| 1747 | H |
| 1748 | I |
| 1749 | K |
| 1750 | L |
| 1751 | M |
| 1752 | N |
| 1753 | O |
| 1754 | P |
| 1755 | Q |
| 1756 | R |
| 1757 | S |
| 1758 | |

| 1759 | A |
|------|---|
| Geo. III. 1760-8 | B |
| 1769 | C |
| 1770 | D |
| 1771 | E |
| 1772 | F |
| 1773 | G |
| 1774 | H |
| 1775 | I |
| 1776 | K |
| 1777 | L |
| 1778 | M |

| 1779 | N | |
|------|---|---|
| 1780 | O | |
| 1781 | P | |
| 1782 | Q | |
| 1783 | R | |
| 1784 | S | |
| 1785 | T | " |
| 1786 | U | |
| 1787 | W | " |
| 1788 | X | " |
| 1789 | Y | " |
| 1790 | Z | " |

| 1791 | A | " |
|------|---|---|
| 1792 | B | " |
| 1793 | C | " |
| 1794 | D | " |
| 1795 | E | " |
| 1796 | F | " |
| 1797 | G | " |
| 1798 | H | " |
| 1799 | I | " |

| 1800 | K | " |
|------|---|---|
| 1801 | L | " |
| 1802 | M | " |
| 1803 | N | |
| 1804 | O | " |
| 1805 | P | " |
| 1806 | Q | " |
| 1807 | R | " |
| 1808 | S | " |
| 1809 | T | " |
| 1810 | U | " |
| 1811 | W | " |
| 1812 | X | " |
| 1813 | Y | " |
| 1814 | Z | " |

# NEWCASTLE

| 1815 | A | ,, | 1839 | A | ,, | 1864 | a | ,, |
|------|---|----|------|---|----|------|---|----|
| 1816 | B | ,, | 1840 | B | ,, | 1865 | b | ,, |
| 1817 | C | ,, | 1841 | C | ☺ | 1866 | c | ,, |
| 1818 | D | ,, | 1842 | D | ,, | 1867 | d | ,, |
| 1819 | E | ,, | 1843 | E | ,, | 1868 | e | ,, |
| Geo IV. 1820 | F | ,, | 1844 | F | ,, | 1869 | f | ,, |
| 1821 | G | ☺ | 1845 | G | ,, | 1870 | g | ,, |
| 1822 | H | ☺ |  |  |  | 1871 | h | ,, |
| 1823 | I | ,, | 1846 | H | ,, | 1872 | i | ,, |
| 1824 | K | ,, | 1847 | I | ,, | 1873 | k | ,, |
| 1825 | L | ,, | 1848 | J | ,, | 1874 | l | ,, |
| 1826 | M | ,, | 1849 | K | ,, | 1875 | m | ,, |
| 1827 | N | ,, | 1850 | L | ,, | 1876 | n | ,, |
| 1828 | O | ,, | 1851 | M | ,, | 1877 | o | ,, |
| 1829 | P | ,, | 1852 | N | ,, | 1878 | p | ,, |
| Wm. IV 1830 | Q | ,, | 1853 | O | ,, | 1879 | q | ,, |
| 1831 | R | ,, | 1854 | P | ,, | 1880 | r | ,, |
| 1832 | S | ☺ | 1855 | Q | ,, | 1881 | s | ,, |
| 1833 | T | ,, | 1856 | R | ,, | 1882 | t | ,, |
| 1834 | U | ,, | 1857 | S | ,, | 1883 | u | ,, |
| 1835 | W | ,, | 1858 | T | ,, |  |  |  |
| 1836 | X | ,, | 1859 | U | ,, |  |  |  |
| Vict. 1837 | Y | ,, | 1860 | W | ,, |  |  |  |
| 1838 | Z | ,, | 1861 | X | ,, |  |  |  |
|  |  |  | 1862 | Y | ,, |  |  |  |
|  |  |  | 1863 | Z | ,, |  |  |  |

# NORWICH

| Year | Mark | Letter | | Year | Mark | Letter |
|------|------|--------|---|------|------|--------|
| 1565 | | A | | | and variations thereof | |
| 1566 | | B | | 1624 | | A |
| 1567 | | C | | 1625 | | B |
| 1568 | | D | | 1626 | | C |
| 1569 | | E | | 1627 | | D |
| 1570 | | F | | 1628 | | E |
| 1571 | " | G | | 1629 | | F |
| 1573 | " | I | | 1630 | | G |
| 1574 | " | K | | 1631 | | H |
| 1579 | | P | | 1632 | | I |
| | | | | 1633 | | K |
| c.1590 | | | | 1634 | | L |
| c.1595 | | | | 1635 | | M |
| c.1600 | | | | 1636 | | N |
| c.1610 | | | | 1637 | | O |
| c.1620 | | | | 1638 | | P |
| | | | | 1639 | | Q |
| | | | | 1640 | | R |
| | | | | 1641 | | S |
| | | | | 1642 | | T |
| | | | | 1643 | | V |

# NORWICH

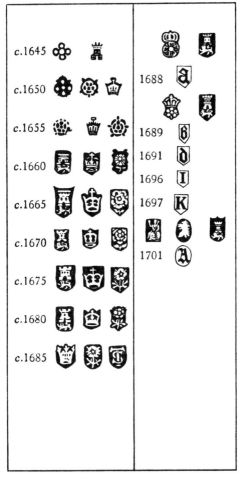

| | | | |
|---|---|---|---|
| c.1645 | | | |
| c.1650 | | | |
| c.1655 | | | |
| c.1660 | | | |
| c.1665 | | | |
| c.1670 | | | |
| c.1675 | | | |
| c.1680 | | | |
| c.1685 | | | |

| | |
|---|---|
| 1688 | |
| 1689 | |
| 1691 | |
| 1696 | |
| 1697 | |
| 1701 | |

# SHEFFIELD

| Year | | | | | Year | | | | |
|------|---|---|---|---|------|---|---|---|---|
| 1773 | | | Œ | | 1798 | | | V | |
| 1774 | | | F | | 1799 | | | E | |
| 1775 | | | N | Mark shown in col. 6 was used on small objects to replace those in 3 and 4 | 1800 | | | N | |
| 1776 | | | R | | 1801 | | | H | |
| 1777 | | | h | | 1802 | | | M | |
| 1778 | | | S | | 1803 | | | F | |
| 1779 | | | A | | 1804 | | | G | |
| 1780 | | | C | | 1805 | | | B | |
| 1781 | | | D | | 1806 | | | A | |
| 1782 | | | G | | 1807 | | | S | |
| 1783 | | | B | | 1808 | | | P | |
| 1784 | | | I | | 1809 | | | K | |
| 1785 | | | P | | 1810 | | | L | |
| 1786 | | | K | | 1811 | | | C | |
| 1787 | | | C | | 1812 | | | D | |
| 1788 | | | u | | 1813 | | | R | |
| 1789 | | | M | | 1814 | | | W | |
| 1790 | | | L | | 1815 | | | O | |
| 1791 | | | P | | 1816 | | | T | |
| 1792 | | | u | | 1817 | | | X | |
| 1793 | | | O | | 1818 | | | I | |
| 1794 | | | m | | 1819 Geo.IV. | | | V | |
| 1795 | | | q | | 1820 | | | Q | |
| 1796 | | | Z | | 1821 | | | Y | |
| 1797 | | | X | | 1822 | | | Z | |

From 15th July, 1797, for nine months, the King's Head was duplicated owing to the Duty being doubled.

# SHEFFIELD

| Year | | | | | | Year | | | |
|------|---|---|---|---|---|------|---|---|---|
| 1823 | 🦀 | 👑 | U | ♛ | U̅ | | 🦀 | 👑 | ◊ |
| 1824 | 🦀 | 👑 | a | ♛ | a | 1848 | E | E♔ | ,, |
| 1825 | 🦀 | 👑 | b | ♛ | b | 1849 | F | F♔ | ,, |
| 1826 | 🦀 | 👑 | c | ♛ | c | 1850 | G | G♔ | ,, |
| 1827 | 🦀 | 👑 | d | ♛ | d | 1851 | H | H♔ | ,, |
| 1828 | 🦀 | 👑 | e | ♛ | e | 1852 | I | I♔ | ,, |
| 1829 Wm. IV. | 🦀 | 👑 | f | ♛ | ♔f | 1853 | K | K♔ | ,, |
| 1830 | 🦀 | 👑 | g | ♛ | ♔g | 1854 | L | ◊ | |
| 1831 | 🦀 | 👑 | h | ♛ | ♔h | 1855 | M | ,, | |
| 1832 | 🦀 | 👑 | k | ♛ | ♔k | 1856 | N | ,, | |
| 1833 | 🦀 | 👑 | l | ♛ | ♔l | 1857 | O | ,, | |
| 1834 | 🦀 | 👑 | m | ♛ | E♔ | 1858 | P | ,, | |
| 1835 | 🦀 | 👑 | p | ♛ | ♔P | 1859 | R | ,, | |
| 1836 Vict. | 🦀 | 👑 | q | ♛ | ♔q | 1860 | S | ,, | |
| 1837 | 🦀 | 👑 | r | ♛ | r♔ | 1861 | T | ,, | |
| 1838 | 🦀 | 👑 | S | ♛ | S♔ | 1862 | U | ,, | |
| 1839 | 🦀 | 👑 | t | ♛ | t♔ | 1863 | V | ,, | |
| 1840 | 🦀 | 👑 | u | ♛ | u♔ | 1864 | W | ,, | |
| 1841 | 🦀 | 👑 | V | ♛ | V♔ | 1865 | X | ,, | |
| 1842 | 🦀 | 👑 | X | ♛ | X♔ | 1866 | Y | ,, | |
| 1843 | 🦀 | 👑 | Z | ♛ | Z♔ | 1867 | Z | ,, | |
| 1844 | 🦀 | 👑 | A | ♛ | A♔ | 1868 | A | ,, | |
| 1845 | 🦀 | 👑 | B | ♛ | B♔ | 1869 | B | ,, | |
| 1846 | 🦀 | 👑 | C | ♛ | C♔ | 1870 | C | ,, | |
| 1847 | 🦀 | 👑 | D | ♛ | D♔ | 1871 | D | ,, | |
| | | | | | | 1872 | E | ,, | |

Mark shown in column 6 was used on small objects to replace those in 3 and 4.

65

# SHEFFIELD

| | | | | | | |
|---|---|---|---|---|---|---|
| 1873 | F | " | 1893 | a | 1914 | w |
| 1874 | G | " | 1894 | b | 1915 | x |
| 1875 | H | " | 1895 | c | 1916 | y |
| 1876 | J | " | 1896 | d | 1917 | z |
| 1877 | K | " | 1897 | e | | |
| 1878 | L | " | 1898 | f | 1918 | a |
| 1879 | M | " | 1899 | g | 1919 | b |
| 1880 | N | " | 1900 | h | 1920 | c |
| 1881 | O | " | Ed. VII 1901 | i | 1921 | d |
| 1882 | P | " | 1902 | k | 1922 | e |
| 1883 | Q | " | 1903 | l | 1923 | f |
| 1884 | R | " | 1904 | m | 1924 | g |
| 1885 | S | " | 1905 | n | 1925 | h |
| 1886 | T | " | 1906 | o | 1926 | i |
| 1887 | U | " | 1907 | p | 1927 | k |
| 1888 | V | " | 1908 | q | 1928 | l |
| 1889 | W | " | 1909 | r | 1929 | m |
| 1890 | X | " | Geo. V 1910 | s | 1930 | n |
| 1891 | Y | | 1911 | t | 1931 | o |
| 1892 | Z | | 1912 | u | 1932 | p |
| | | | 1913 | v | | |

# SHEFFIELD

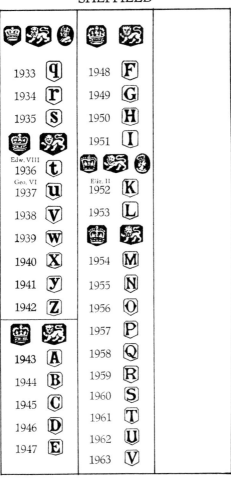

| Year | Mark | Year | Mark |
|------|------|------|------|
| 1933 | q | 1948 | F |
| 1934 | r | 1949 | G |
| 1935 | s | 1950 | H |
| Edw. VIII 1936 | t | 1951 | I |
| Geo. VI 1937 | u | Eliz. II 1952 | K |
| 1938 | v | 1953 | L |
| 1939 | w | 1954 | M |
| 1940 | X | 1955 | N |
| 1941 | y | 1956 | O |
| 1942 | Z | 1957 | P |
| 1943 | A | 1958 | Q |
| 1944 | B | 1959 | R |
| 1945 | C | 1960 | S |
| 1946 | D | 1961 | T |
| 1947 | E | 1962 | U |
|      |   | 1963 | V |

# YORK

| From about 1560 to 1606 variations of | From about 1560 to 1606 variations of | 1607 to 1630 varies between |
|---|---|---|
| 🔵 (1568) | 🔵 (1583) | 🔵 (1608)  🔵 (1624) |
| | | 1607 — a |
| 🔵 (1577) | 🔵 (1594) | 1608 — b |
| | | 1609 — c |
| | | 1610 — d |
| | | 1611 — e |
| Eliz. | 1583 — a | 1612 — f |
| | 1584 — b | 1613 — g |
| 1564 — F | 1587 — e | 1614 — h |
| 1565 — G | 1590 — h | 1615 — i |
| 1566 — H | 1592 — k | 1616 — k |
| 1568 — K | 1593 — l | 1617 — l |
| 1569 — L | 1594 — m | 1618 — m |
| 1570 — M | 1595 — n | 1619 — n |
| 1572 — O | 1596 — o | 1620 — o |
| 1573 — P | 1597 — p | 1621 — p |
| 1574 — Q | 1598 — q | 1622 — q |
| 1575 — R | 1599 — r | 1623 — r |
| 1576 — S | 1601 — t | 1624 — s |
| 1577 — T | Jas. I | Chas. l. |
| 1582 — Z | 1604 — x | 1625 — t |
| | | 1626 — u |
| | | 1627 — w |
| | | 1628 — x |
| | | 1629 — y |
| | | 1630 — z |

# YORK

| 1631 to 1656 | 1657 to 1681 | 1682 to 1699 |
|---|---|---|
| | | (1680) (1696) |
| 1631 *a* | 1657 Ⓐ | 1682 Ⓐ |
| 1632 *b* | 1658 Ⓑ | 1683 Ⓑ |
| 1633 *c* | 1659 Ⓒ | 1684 Ⓒ |
| 1634 *d* | Chas. II | Jas. II |
| 1635 *e* | 1660 Ⓓ | 1685 Ⓓ |
| 1636 *f* | 1661 Ⓔ | 1686 Ⓔ |
| 1637 *g* | 1662 Ⓕ | 1687 Ⓕ |
| 1638 *h* | 1663 Ⓖ | 1688 Ⓖ |
| 1639 *i* | 1664 Ⓗ | Wm. & My. |
| 1641 *k* | 1665 Ⓙ | 1689 Ⓗ |
| 1642 *l* | 1666 Ⓚ | 1690 Ⓙ |
| 1643 *m* | 1667 Ⓛ | 1691 Ⓚ |
| 1645 Comwth 1649 *o* | 1668 Ⓜ | 1692 Ⓛ |
| 1650 *t* | 1669 Ⓝ | 1693 Ⓜ |
| 1651 *u* | 1670 Ⓞ | 1694 Ⓝ |
| 1652 *v* | 1671 Ⓟ | 1695 Wm. III 1696 Ⓞ |
| 1653 *w* | 1672 Ⓠ | 1697 Ⓠ |
| 1654 *x* | 1673 Ⓡ | 1698 Ⓡ |
| 1655 *y* | 1674 Ⓢ | 1699 Ⓢ |
| 1656 *z* | 1675 Ⓣ | |
| | 1677 Ⓥ | |
| | 1678 Ⓦ | |
| | 1679 Ⓧ | |
| | 1680 Ⓨ | |
| | 1681 Ⓩ | |

# YORK

| 🛡 👑 🦁 | ⊕ 🦁 🛡 👤 | ⊕ 🦁 👑 🦁 |
|---|---|---|
| 1700 **Ꭱ** | 1787 **A** " | 1812 **a** .. |
| 1701 **B** | 1788 **B** " | 1813 **b** .. |
| Anne 1702 **C** | 1789 **C** or **C** " | 1814 **c** " |
| 1703 **D** | 1790 **d** " | 1815 **d** " |
| 1705 **F** | 1791 **e** " | 1816 **e** " |
| 1706 **G** | 1792 **f** " | 1817 **f** " |
| 1708 **ᚺ** | 1793 **g** " | 1818 **g** " |
| 1711 **ᛗ** | 1794 **h** " | 1819 Geo. IV 1820 **h** " |
| 1713 **ᛟ** | 1795 **i** " | 1820 **i** " |
| | 1796 **k** 🦁 | 1821 **k** " |
| No plate yet found bearing date letter between 1713 to 1778 | 1797 **L** " | 1822 **l** " |
| | 1798 **M** " | 1823 **m** " |
| | 1799 **N** " | 1824 **n** " |
| | 1800 **O** " | 1825 **o** " |
| 🛡 🦁 👑 | 1801 **P** " | 1826 **p** " |
| Geo. III. 1778 **C** | 1802 **Q** " | 1827 **q** " |
| 1779 **D** | 1803 **R** " | 1828 **r** " |
| 1780 **E** | 1804 **S** " | 1829 **s** " |
| 1781 **F** | 1805 **T** " | Wm. IV 1830 **t** 👑 |
| 1782 **G** | 1806 **U** " | 1831 **u** " |
| 1783 **H** | 1807 **V** " | 1832 **v** " |
| 1784 **J** 🛡 | 1808 **W** " | 1833 **w** " |
| 1785 **K** " | 1809 **X** " | 1834 **x** " |
| 1786 **L** 👑 | 1810 **Y** " | 1835 **y** " |
| | 1811 **Z** " | 1836 **3** " |
| | 🦁 Lion found for 1803 & 1806 facing right | |

70

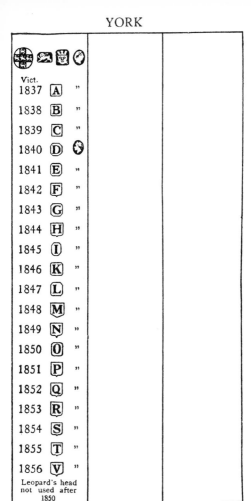

| Vict. | | |
|---|---|---|
| 1837 | **A** | ,, |
| 1838 | **B** | ,, |
| 1839 | **C** | ,, |
| 1840 | **D** | ⊕ |
| 1841 | **E** | ,, |
| 1842 | **F** | ,, |
| 1843 | **G** | ,, |
| 1844 | **H** | ,, |
| 1845 | **I** | ,, |
| 1846 | **K** | ,, |
| 1847 | **L** | ,, |
| 1848 | **M** | ,, |
| 1849 | **N** | ,, |
| 1850 | **O** | ,, |
| 1851 | **P** | ,, |
| 1852 | **Q** | ,, |
| 1853 | **R** | ,, |
| 1854 | **S** | ,, |
| 1855 | **T** | ,, |
| 1856 | **V** | ,, |

Leopard's head
not used after
1850

# MARKS USED BY MINOR GUILDS

## ENGLAND

Barnstaple . about 1370 to about 1730

Bristol . . . 1730 ,, 1800

Hull. . . . . 1570 ,, 1710

King's Lynn 1600 ,, 1700

Leeds . . . . 1650 ,, 1700

Lincoln . . . 1420 ,, 1710

Plymouth . 1600 ,, 1700

Taunton . . 1640 ,, 1700

## SCOTLAND

Aberdeen . 1450 ,, 1880

Arbroath . . 1830 ,, 1840

Banff . . . . 1680 ,, 1850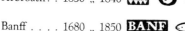

Canongate . 1600 ,, 1836
(Edinburgh)

Dundee . . . 1550 ,, 1834

Elgin . . . . 1700 ,, 1830

SCOTLAND—continued

Greenock . 1745 „ 1825

Inverness . . about 1640 to about 1880

Montrose . 1650 „ 1820

Perth . . . . 1550 „ 1850

Tain . . 1720 „ 1800

Wick . . . . 1780 „ 1820

IRELAND

Cork . . 1660 „ 1840

Galway . 1640 „ 1750

Kilkenny 1650 „ 1700

Limerick . 1700 „ 1800

Youghal . . 1650 „ 1720

<u>CHANNEL ISLANDS</u>
Guernsey.. 1690 ,, 1750

Jersey..... 1760 ,, 1830

<u>SOUTH AFRICA</u>
Cape of Good Hope, 1715 to 1790

<u>JAMAICA</u>
1800 ,,

# GOLD MARKING

FROM 1300 the standard for gold was 19¼ carats and until 1363 the leopard's head was the only assay mark struck on gold. In 1363 the maker's mark was introduced and in 1478 the date letter was added. In 1477 the standard was reduced to 18 carat and in 1575 raised to 22 carat. In 1544 the lion passant replaced the leopard's head as the standard mark. In 1798 the 18 carat standard was reintroduced additional to the 22 carat and the crown mark used in place of the lion passant, the latter, remaining the distinguishing mark for 22 carat until 1844 when the crown was used for both and the lion passant discarded.

In 1854 three lower standards were introduced, 15, 12, and 9, which had no standard mark other than the carat numbers and the carat value in decimals.

In 1932 the 15 and 12 carats were discontinued and a new standard of 14 carat was substituted.

22 carat      18 carat

14 carat      9 carat

Gold standard marks from 1932 onwards.

In addition to these distinguishing marks for gold the articles must also be struck with the town mark, date letter and maker's mark, and between the years 1784 and 1890 the Sovereign's head was struck to indicate that duty had been paid. In Sheffield the town mark for silver is the crown, so for gold it substitutes a York rose which is stamped on all gold wares of whatever carat. In addition the crown is punched on 22 and 18 carat gold only as at other English assay offices. Gold was not assayed in Sheffield before 1905.

Table of principle changes in standard.

| 1300 to 1476 | 🛡️ | | indicating 19½ carat |
| 1477 to 1544 | ,, | ,, | 18 ,, |
| 1544 to 1574 | 🦁 | ,, | 18 ,, |
| 1575 to 1797 | ,, | ,, | 22 ,, |
| 1798 to 1843 | ,, | ,, | 22 ,, |
| and | 👑 **18** | ,, | 18 ,, |
| 1844 to 1853 | ,, 22 | ,, | 22 ,, |
| | ,, 18 | ,, | 18 ,, |
| 1854 to 1931 | ,, 22 | ,, | 22 ,, |
| | ,, 18 | ,, | 18 ,, |
| | 15 (·625) ,, | | 15 ,, |
| | 12 (·5) ,, | | 12 ,, |
| | 9 (·375) ,, | | 9 ,, |
| 1932 to date | 👑 **22** | ,, | 22 ,, |
| | ,, 18 | ,, | 18 ,, |
| | 14 (·585) ,, | | 14 ,, |
| | 9 (·375) ,, | | 9 ,, |

IN Dublin the standards are 22, 20 (rarely),
18, 14, 12 and 9 carats, Until 1784 the same
marks were used as for silver, the standard
being 22 carat In 1784 the marks for 22 carat
became

 date
letter   maker's
mark

at the same time a 20 carat standard was introduced with the following additional marks

🌸 **20**

also 18 carat with a unicorn's head erased and

the figure 18  🦄 **18**  The crowned harp

was omitted from jewellery and also from the
lower standards, 15, 12, and 9 carats.

# MARKS ON IMPORTED PLATE

THE Customs Act of 1842 made illegal the selling of imported plate either gold or silver in Great Britain and Ireland unless it had been assayed at a British office. In 1867 the F Mark was introduced as

**F** **F**

an addition to the appropriate British Hall Marks.

FOREIGN Plate made prior to 1800 was exempted by the Customs (Amendment) Act of 1842. The Hallmarking of Foreign Plate Act of 1939 exempted foreign plate which was more than 100 years old. Articles of foreign plate which in the opinion of the Commissioners of Customs may be properly described as hand chased, inlaid, bronzed or filigree work of Oriental pattern are exempted by the Revenue Act of 1884.

IN 1904 it was enacted by Order in Council that the carat value of gold should be shown.

| | | | |
|---|---|---|---|
| 22 carat | **22 ·916** | 22 carat | **22 ·916** |
| 20 carat | **20 ·833** | 18 carat | **18 ·750** |
| 18 carat | **18 ·75** | 14 carat | **14 ·585** |
| 15 carat | **15 ·625** | 9 carat | **9 ·375** |
| 12 carat | **12 ·5** | | Gold standard marks from 1932 onwards |
| 9 carat | **9 ·375** | | |

Gold standard marks from 1904 to 1932

BY the same order foreign silver had to be marked the decimal value of the standard used.

| | | | |
|---|---|---|---|
| Sterling Standard | **·925** | Britannia Standard | **·9584** |

77

IN addition the annual date letter and a special assay office mark had to be struck. The F mark was omitted.

SOME of these marks were altered again by Order in Council in May 1906 and in August, 1932.

THE shield containing the Assay Offices Mark for gold is always in a Square with chamfered corners and for silver in a blunt oval.

| Assay Office | Period | Gold Mark | Silver Mark |
|---|---|---|---|
| London | 1904-06 | | |
| | 1906-to date | | |
| Birmingham | 1904-to date | | |
| Chester | 1904-62 | | |
| Dublin | 1904-06 | | |
| | 1906-to date | | |
| Edinburgh | 1904-to date | | |
| Glasgow | 1904-06 | | |
| | 1906-to date | | |
| Sheffield | 1904-06 | | |
| | 1906-to date | | |

## Old Sheffield Plate

FOR full particulars of the craft and general information, see *History of Old Sheffield Plate*, by Frederick Bradbury (published by Macmillan & Co. Ltd., 1912); also *Old Silver Platers and their Marks*, by B. W. Watson, M.A., Sheffield Assay Office.

# SHEFFIELD PLATE

is the term used to denote articles made of copper coated with silver by fusion, invented in 1742 by Thomas Boulsover  This process lapsed on the introduction of the method of silver-plating by electro-deposition about the middle of the 19th century.

## MARKS

THESE can be divided into three groups and will be of great assistance to collectors as a means of identifying both the period and maker of a specimen bearing marks.  Though of great use as a general guide, these marks cannot be relied upon for absolute accuracy of date owing to the absence of any date letters associated with the makers' marks.

## GROUP I.

THE earliest record of a mark probably synchronizes with the first production of Joseph Hancock

circa 1755 **IH** his initial punch closely resembled

the contemporary London silversmiths' punches

A few years later we find **ℒ** Law's initials.

associated with his full name **TH° LAW** Then

H. Tudor's device 1760 **HT** repeated three times,

more closely resembling the marks on solid silver articles than former representations. This marking of earlier made Sheffield Plate terminated in 1772, owing to successful agitation by London silversmiths.

## GROUP II.

BY the year 1784, the Sheffield Plate manufacturers were successful in obtaining an Act which authorized their marking of goods with a device associated with the maker's name

These regulations, however, were not very strictly adhered to and we find many examples where the registered mark appears unassociated with name of maker; this, in fact, became the more frequent form of marking early in the 19th century.

## GROUP III.

ABOUT the year 1805, there suddenly sprang into use a large quantity of spoons, forks, dessert knives, fish servers, skewers, and many other articles described as "flat ware" for domestic use. The surface was plated with thin sheets of silver attached thereto by solder; this process was described as "close plating." As the origin of this method was associated with the town of Birmingham, it will be found that a great influx of makers' marks was registered in Sheffield by the producers of Close Plate in that town in the year 1807.

By the Act of 1784, any maker of goods plated with silver or made to look like silver, within 100 miles of Sheffield, who desired to place a mark thereon had to register the same at the Sheffield Silver Assay Office, and Birmingham makers consequently came within the scope of this Act.

THE last registration of marks recorded for either Sheffield Plate or Close Plated articles at the Sheffield Office was in the year 1836.

THE Crown as a mark was used frequently between the years 1765 and 1825 by various makers as a guarantee of quality.

## OLD SHEFFIELD PLATE MARKS
and those struck on Silver-plated Steel
Cutlery described as "Close Plate."

| Date | Name of Firm | Makers' Marks |
|------|--------------|---------------|
| 1743 | Boulsover Thomas.. | No Mark Traced |
| 1755 | Hancock Joseph ... | IOSᴴ HANCOCK SHEFFIELD. **IH** |
| 1756 | Smith Nathaniel ... | **NS** |
| 1758 | Law Thomas ... | 𝕳 THᵒ LAW 𝕳 / 𝕳 **LAW** 𝕳 |
| 1760 | Tudor & Leader .. | 𝓚 T&Cᵒ / 𝕳 𝕳 𝕳 / 𝕳 𝕳 𝕳 |
| 1760 | Fenton Matthew&Co | 𝕭 𝕭 𝕭 𝕭 |
| 1760 | Unidentified ... | 𝕹 𝕹 𝕹 |
| 1760 | Unidentified ... | 𝕬 𝕬 𝕬 |
| 1760 | Unidentified .. | 𝕸 𝕸 𝕸 𝕸 |
| 1764 | Hoyland John & Co | 𝕳 𝕳 𝕳 𝕳 / 𝕵 𝕳 𝕳 𝕲 |
| 1764 | Boulton & Fothergill | 🙂 **B&F** 🙂 |
| 1765 | Roberts Jacob & Samuel | **JSR** |

| | | |
|---|---|---|
| 1765 | Winter John & Co | |
| 1765 | Morton Richard .. | |
| 1768 | Rowbotham J. & Co | |
| 1770 | Ashforth, Ellis & Co | |
| 1770 | Ryland William .. | No Mark Traced. |
| 1772 | Littlewood J. .. | PLATED |

No marks legalized between 1773 and 1784

| | | |
|---|---|---|
| 1784 | Ashforth G. & Co. .. | |
| 1784 | Fox T. & Co. ... .. | |
| 1784 | Green W. & Co. ... | |
| 1784 | Holy D., Wilkinson & Co | |
| 1784 | Law T. & Co. ... .. | |
| 1784 | Parsons J. & Co. ... .. | |
| 1784 | Smith N. & Co. ... .. | |
| 1784 | Staniforth, Parkin & Co. | |
| 1784 | Sykes & Co. ... .. | |
| 1784 | Tudor, Leader & Nicholson | |

| 1784 | Boulton M. & Co. | .. | |
| 1784 | Dixon T & Co . | . | |
| 1784 | Holland H & Co. | | |
| 1784 | Moore J. ... ... | . | |
| 1784 | Smith & Co. | .. | |
| 1785 | Beldon, Hoyland & Co.. | | |
| 1785 | Brittain, Wilkinson & Brownill | | |
| 1785 | Deakin, Smith & Co . | | |
| 1785 | Love J. & Co. ... (Love, Silverside, Darby & Co ) | | |
| 1785 | Morton R. & Co. | . | |
| 1785 | Roberts, Cadman & Co | | |
| 1786 | Roberts J. & S. ... | | |
| 1786 | Sutcliffe R. & Co. | . | |
| 1787 | Bingley W. ... | . | |
| 1788 | Madin F. & Co. ... | | |
| 1789 | Jervis W ... | | |

| 1790 | Colmore S. ... .. | |
| 1794 | Goodwin E. ... .. | |
| 1795 | Watson, Fenton & Bradbury | |
| 1797 | Froggatt, Coldwell & Lean | |
| 1799 | Green J. & Co. ... .. | |
| 1800 | Goodman, Gainsford & Fairbairn | |
| 1803 | Ellerby W. ... .. | |
| 1803 | Garnett W. ... .. | |
| 1804 | Holy D., Parker & Co. .. | |
| 1804 | Newbould W. & Son . | |
| 1805 | Drabble I. & Co. . | |
| 1806 | Coldwell W. ... . | |
| 1806 | Hill D. & Co. ... . | |
| 1807 | Law J. & Son ... . | |
| 1807 | Butts T. ... . | |
| 1807 | Green J. ... . | |

# OLD SHEFFIELD PLATE

| 1807 | Hutton W. ... ... | |
|------|------|------|
| 1807 | Law R. ... ... ... | |
| 1807 | Linwood J. ... ... | |
| 1807 | Linwood W. ... ... | |
| 1807 | Meredith H. ... ... | |
| 1807 | Peake ... ... ... | |
| 1807 | Ryland W. & Son ... | |
| 1807 | Scot W ... ... | |
| 1807 | Silkirk W ... ... | |
| 1807 | Thomason E. & Dowler... | |
| 1807 | Tonks Samuel .. ... | |
| 1807 | Waterhouse & Co. .. | |
| 1807 | Wilmore Joseph .. | |
| 1808 | Gainsford R. ... .. | |
| 1808 | Hatfield A. ... .. | |
| 1808 | Banister W. ... .. | |

# OLD SHEFFIELD PLATE

| | | | |
|------|------------------------------|------|---|
| 1808 | Gibbs G. | ... | .. |
| 1808 | Hipkiss J. | ... | .. |
| 1808 | Horton D. | ... | .. |
| 1808 | Lea A. C. | ... | .. |
| 1808 | Linwood M. & Sons | .. | |
| 1808 | Nicholds J. | ... | .. |
| 1809 | Beldon G. | ... | .. |
| 1809 | Wright J. & Fairbairn G | | |
| 1809 | Cheston T. | ... | .. |
| 1809 | Harrison J. | ... | .. |
| 1809 | Hipwood W. | ... | .. |
| 1809 | Horton J. | ... | .. |
| 1809 | Silk R. ... | ... | .. |
| 1809 | Howard S. & T. ... | | |
| 1810 | Smith, Tate, Nicholson & Hoult | | |
| 1810 | Dunn G. B. | ... | .. |
| 1810 | Hanson M. | ... | ... |
| 1810 | Pimley S. | ... | ... |

87

# OLD SHEFFIELD PLATE

| 1811 | Creswick T. & J. | .. | CRESWICKS |
| 1811 | Stot B. ... ... | .. | Stot |
| 1811 | Watson, Pass & Co. (late J. Watson) | | WATSON PASS & Cº |
| 1811 | Lees G. ... ... | .. | LEES |
| 1811 | Pearson R. ... | .. | PEARSON |
| 1811 | White J. (White & Allgood) | | WHITE |
| 1812 | Kirkby S. ... | .. | KIRKBY FOR·USE |
| 1812 | Allgood J. ... | .. | ALL GOOD |
| 1812 | Allport E. ... | .. | Allport |
| 1812 | Gilbert J. ... | .. | Gilbert |
| 1812 | Hinks J. ... | .. | HINKS |
| 1812 | Johnson J. ... | .. | JOHNSON |
| 1812 | Small T. ... ... | .. | SMALL |
| 1812 | Smith W. ... | .. | SMITH |
| 1813 | Younge S. & C. & Co. .. | | S.C. YOUNGE & Cº |
| 1813 | Thomas S. ... | .. | THOMAS |
| 1813 | Tyndall J. ... | .. | TYNDALL |
| 1814 | Best H. ... ... | .. | BEST |
| 1814 | Cracknall J. ... | .. | CRACKNALL |

| 1814 | Jordan T. ... ... | |
| 1814 | Woodward W. ... .. | |
| 1815 | Lilly John .. .. | |
| 1816 | Best & Wastidge .. | |
| 1816 | Ashley ... .. .. | |
| 1816 | Davis J. ... .. | |
| 1816 | Evans S. .. .. | |
| 1816 | Freeth H. ... .. | |
| 1816 | Harwood T. ... .. | |
| 1816 | Lilly Joseph ... .. | |
| 1816 | Turley S. ... .. | |
| 1817 | Cope C. G. ... .. | |
| 1817 | Pemberton & Mitchell .. | |
| 1817 | Shephard J. ... .. | |
| 1818 | Markland W. ... .. | |
| 1819 | Corn J. & J. Sheppard.. | |
| 1819 | Rogers J. ... .. | |

| 1820 | Hall W. ... ... .. | |
| 1820 | Moore F. ... .. | |
| 1820 | Turton J. ... .. | |
| 1821 | Blagden, Hodgson & Co. | |
| 1821 | Holy D. & G. ... .. | |
| 1821 | Needham C. ... .. | |
| 1821 | Sansom T. & Sons .. | |
| 1821 | Child T. ... ... .. | |
| 1821 | Smith I. ... ... .. | |
| 1821 | Worton S. ... .. | |
| 1822 | Rodgers J. & Sons .. | |
| 1822 | Bradshaw J. ... .. | |
| 1823 | Briggs W. ... .. | |
| 1823 | Harrison G. ... .. | |
| 1823 | Smallwood J. ... .. | |
| 1824 | Causer J. F. ... .. | |

| 1824 | Jones ... ... .. | |
| 1824 | Tonks & Co. ... .. | |
| 1828 | Roberts, Smith & Co. .. | |
| 1828 | Smith J. & Son ... .. | |
| 1828 | Askew ... ... .. | A SKEW MAKER NOTTINGHAM |
| 1829 | Hall Henry ... ... | |
| 1829 | Hobday J. ... .. | |
| 1830 | Watson J. & Son .. | |
| 1830 | Bishop Thomas... .. | |
| 1831 | Hutton W. ... .. | |
| 1833 | Atkin Henry ... .. | |
| 1833 | Waterhouse I. & I. & Co. | |
| 1833 | Watson W. ... .. | WWATSON MAKER SHEFFIELD |
| 1835 | Dixon J. & Sons .. | |

| | | |
|---|---|---|
| 1836 | Smith J. ... .. | |
| 1836 | Waterhouse, Hatfield & Co. | |
| 1836 | Wilkinson H. & Co. .. | |
| 1837 | Hutton W. ... .. | |
| 1839 | Hutton W. ... .. | |
| 1839 | Prime J. ... .. | |
| 1840 | Walker, Knowles & Co. | |
| 1842 | Waterhouse George & Co | |
| 1848 | Smith, Sissons & Co. .. | |
| 1849 | Padley, Parkin & Co. .. | |
| 1849 | Hutton W. ... .. | |
| 1850 | Mappin Bros. ... .. | |
| 1860 | Oldham T. ... .. | |
| 1860 | Roberts & Briggs. .. | |

FROM 1840 to 1860 nickel silver gradually superseded the use of copper, and articles were produced by the aid of both processes: though the bodies of larger pieces continued to be constructed of fused plated metal. the other parts were subjected to the process of electro deposition.

# OLD SHEFFIELD PLATE

THE following marks have been used extensively in recent times on nickel silver articles plated by the process of electro-deposition.

The Bell     The Hand     The Cross Arrows

The Pineapple     The Cross Keys

— ◆ —

DEVICES on Plated articles, as illustrated above, were in vogue after the cessation of registrations of Sheffield Plate Marks at the Sheffield Office. As they too closely resembled the Sheffield Silver Assay Marks, the use of the Crown was prohibited in 1896.

J. W. Northend Ltd., Printers & Publishers
Sheffield, England, 1964

# NOTES

# NOTES

# NOTES